The Sweetness and the Pits

Remembrances of a Georgia Peach

LYNNE BARFIELD BYRD

The author has tried to recreate events, locations, and conversations from personal memories. In some instances, in order to maintain their anonymity, some individuals' identifying characteristics and details of their lives and our interactions have been changed while remaining true to the essence of the story.

Editing, writer's coaching, and project management:
Wayne South Smith, www.waynesouthsmith.com

Cover photo restoration by Laura Nalesnik, www.mousewhiskers.com

Quote by Elsie de Wolfe on page 8 from her book *The House in Good Taste*, The Century Company, Hard Press Publishing and Rizzoli Publishing

Ballet In The Fifties by Janice Townley Moore on page 85, used with permission from the author and Old Mountain Press

Excerpt from *Prayer, Stress and Inner Wounds* by Flora Slosson Wuellner on page 253, The Upper Room Press

Photos and artworks courtesy of Noah Byrd, Lynne Byrd, members of the Bella Literati Book Club, other family and friends, as well as:

"Tea at Dunwoody Farmhouse" on page 3, featured in *North Point* magazine, used with permission of Haigwood Studios, Roswell, Georgia

"Duck and Cover" and "Dog Tags" on page 76, copyright by Daily Republic, Inc., www.dailyrepublic.com

"David Patrick, Guitar Soloist" on page 138, from Confidante Cassettes

"Dunwoody Farmhouse to be replaced by all-night gas station" on page 202, watercolor by Bob Cargill, published in *The Dunwoody Crier* newspaper, 1996

Dunwoody United Methodist Church stage production photos on pages 206–207 by DUMC member Carrie Brown.

ISBN: 978-0-692-49548-3

To my husband, Noah

And

To the memory of

The Morningside Mothers

Contents

1   I'm So Glad You're Here!. 1

2   How I Got My Name 9

3   A Big Loving Family. 13

4   Ancestry 17

5   My Parents' Marriage: An Unlikely Romance 23

6   Pearl Harbor 29

7   The 40s 31

8   After the War 35

9   Uncle Honey and Aunt Bee. 39

10   Growing Up in Virginia Highlands. 45

11   Blackstone the Magician and His "Plant" 61

12   The Morningside Experience. 65

13   Books, Ailments, and "Duck and Cover" 73

14   What is Normal? A Continuing Nightmare 77

15   Jarene Townlovska and Lene Barfilova, Future Ballerinas . . . 83

16   Camp Toccoa 87

17   Christmas 89

18   The Morningside Mothers. 95

19   The Fabulous 50s 99

20   Real and Imagined Careers 111

21   Marrying My Childhood Sweetheart 119

22   Babies Having Babies, Part #1 .123

23   Babies Having Babies, Part #2. 127

24   Trouble 141

25   The Funeral and a Heavenly Visit 145

26   Transitional Time 149

27   Mr. Right 153

28   Life on Spalding Drive with the Crew. 159

29   The Other Woman 163

30   The "Not a Christian" Thing. .177

31   A New Career for Us. 181

32   My Bucket List 189

33   The Dunwoody Preservation Trust 199

34   Church Drama 205

35   Fabulous Trips. 209

36   Precious Pets 215

37   Very Special Family and Friends 223

38   The Bella Literati Book Club. .239

39   Looking Ahead 249

40   Staying Strong. 253

Acknowledgements *257*

About the Author. *259*

CHAPTER 1

I'm So Glad You're Here!

I'm Southern through and through. What an interesting and wonderful ride it has been. I've always felt that I was a late bloomer or maybe born too late, and that I would have made a great Southern Belle in the 19th Century, as fond as I am of antiques and preservation. Of course I would have been very rich...!

A few years ago I put together a small spiral bound book for my children, my grandchildren, and my brother's children. I avoided any unpleasant or dark times in our lives, but now I'm ready to share them. Nobody is left alive who can get their feelings hurt, and this memoir is for a larger audience, which includes me. You may think certain people you know have no worries and no conflict in their lives, but once you get to know them well, you realize that we all have trips down in the valley and mountain top experiences too.

1

Everybody has a story to tell—you do too! Some memories are as sweet as a ripe peach. Others are like the juice that dribbles onto your chin, which then needs a good washing, or like the pit that you're done with. As my Aunt Bee used to say, I am thrilled "twist-legged" to share my story with you, and I'll include the "sweet, ripe peach" times *and* the "pits."

Time has given me a perspective that would have been impossible when I was young. Everything in my story is just as I remember it. Even the short story I have included about my husband's "Other Woman" is true except for the ending. If there is one word that I would hope describes me, it would be "authentic."

I have told my husband that if I go first to be sure and say that I loved being Southern in my obituary. And if he goes first, at least this book can testify for me!

Writing this has been a catharsis for me, but most of all, I hope you find pleasure in reading it.

Now, I'm just going to assume that you don't know a thing about being Southern, so please forgive me if you are insulted with what you already know!

There is a very good reason why most Southerners value hospitality. In plantation days, the homes and properties were very far apart. Few people visited, and when they did, they were eagerly welcomed. We are also slower in our speech—and usually in everything. The Old South was hot and the New South still is! Just take your time!

Since I am from Atlanta, many would say that there is a definite Atlanta accent which is very different from Hollywood's

JOYCE AMACHER AND LYNNE BYRD HAVING TEA AT THE
HISTORIC DUNWOODY FARMHOUSE, DECEMBER 2002

idea of a Southern drawl. It is much more understated. According to Allyn Partin, a dialect coach who has worked with actors, "there is a musicality to an Atlanta accent. The vowels are more rounded." Another prominent quality is what she calls "r-deletion." This is when an "r" follows a vowel, the "r" is either not pronounced or minimally pronounced, such as "opportunity" becomes "opp-ah-toon-i-ty," or "whatever" becomes "what-eh-vah." She says that when she works with actors who need to use a Southern accent, she just tells them to drop the "r."

I'm not an expert on accents—I would like to be—but I know from my studies of Anthropology and Folklore that language is learned early, and accents and colloquialisms all are important to a culture. There is no wrong way to speak your own language. Most Native Georgians are from the Piedmont area; Piedmont means "foot of the rock." The

Georgia Piedmont lies between the Blue Ridge Mountains and the Upper Coastal Plain, being part of a larger area called the southern Piedmont, which is in the southeastern and mid-Atlantic regions of the United States. European settlement patterns and Native American settlement patterns made all the difference in "handed down" accents.

Because of the influx of other cultures into Atlanta, the true Atlanta accent is becoming very rare. I hope this doesn't hurt anyone's feelings, for goodness sakes. You can't help it if your family is or isn't from the South. Just be who you are. Everybody else is already taken.

One thing I do know is that you get more of what you want with "shugah" than with "vinegah." Now truth be told, not all Southern gals are manipulators like Scarlett O'Hara. Gals known as "Steel Magnolias" get a lot done, and we need them, but there is nothing soft about them.

Pretending was traditionally what Southerners my age did during a crisis or any unpleasantness in the family, at times to their own detriment. I'm sure this also made a difference in the way that I and many other Southerners react to life, even now. We treat the strange, the alcoholic, or mentally ill members of our family as "different" or "eccentric," and we try not to "air the dirty laundry." Our unspoken motto is "Unpleasant things are best not talked about."

Still, Southern Belles are strong, although some are not steely. My sister-in-law Colleen shared that her grandmother would tell her, "When your husband says something ugly or hurts your feelings, you just pinch your finger." There was no limit of hurts for her grandmother. However, Colleen says that even as a young girl she knew she was not going to be the "pinch your finger" type. Although she has spent much of her adult life in Florida, her heritage is Southern, and she is definitely a charming Southern Belle, and, when required, a Steel Magnolia. She was a "soulmate" for me from the start of our friendship.

When I first met Colleen, I loved her because she loved my brother Larry. After I got to know her, it didn't take long before I just plain loved her for herself.

Colleen is a great example of the southern girl who always looks her best. This is passed from southern mother to southern girls, the first advice of which is to always wear clean underwear "because you might be in an accident." Along with looking your best, you are reminded to remember "who you are," whatever that really means. Colleen always has perfect make-up, luxurious eyelashes, lovely teeth, a beautiful smile, and every hair in its place. And this could be at 7:00 a.m. when she is in charge of a women's group at church. It used to be my opinion that southern women were more beautiful than women from the north. My husband still thinks so...but when you think about it, why put on a full face of makeup in the winter when snow is blowing in it and you are mostly hidden by your parka, and you are freezing to boot?

This "looking your best" thing has always been a part of a daily ritual no matter what my schedule is. One winter we did have an ice storm and lost our electricity. The neighbors were gathering outside to check on whether or not everyone was okay. I had to take time to get out three candles so I could put on my makeup. This is something that I do for myself, not others. This includes make-up for exercise class, raking leaves in the yard, or cleaning the house.

Southern women also *love* to shop. Once, when Colleen and Larry were visiting, we spent the whole day shopping. Colleen has always thought that Atlanta has an advantage over Miami when it comes to interesting places to shop. Toward the end of the afternoon, I was beginning to have a sinking spell, and I asked Colleen if she would like to take a break and stop for some coffee and a rest. She said, "Oh no! I'm fine! I've been trained by professionals!"

Before I forget it, I need to mention that most Southern women have a string of lovely pearls, sometimes the only nice piece of jewelry they have. When each one of my grand-daughters graduated from high school, I gave them a nice pearl necklace and told them that it would always give them confidence. Remember, we are instructed from the start not to forget who we are. Additionally, I gave each of them a glass doorknob to remind them that as they grow up, some doors will close for them, but new doors will open, and this is all good.

In my opinion, growing up Southern is a privilege, and as such, we are expected to be hospitable and kind. We will bring you food and clean your house if you have a death in the family, and maybe we'll bring your folks a lemonade cake for when they get to your house after the funeral.

If you are Southern, when you were growing up and needed a spanking, your Mama or Daddy probably told you to "Go out in the yard and pick me a switch." The switch was expected to be long enough to hurt your legs when you got your switchin'. If the switch was not adequate, you were sent back outside to find one that was. It was a challenge to find one that fit the bill but didn't hurt too much.

Most women in the South are good loyal friends. To eat, we favor fried chicken, collards with pot likker, grits, sweet potatoes, banana pudding, and either sweet tea or Coca-Cola to drink. Since we have learned more about diets, some of us have backed off from some of the sugary drinks and cholesterol-producing dishes. Our grandmothers didn't know anything about bacon drippins' causing high cholesterol. But, for sure, it's hard to cook a pot of collards without at least a hint of bacon drippings. Also, most of the Southern women I know have a sweet tooth. I wonder if this could be genetic.

I'm sorry to say that you can't *become* Southern. One of my pet peeves is a movie star trying to have a Southern accent. God give me strength! I can't stand it!

However, if you weren't fortunate enough to be born in the South, this quote by Elsie de Wolfe will get you close to the true Southern stuff. Miss de Wolfe, the author of *The House in Good Taste,* a woman who gained the title of "America's first interior designer" and threw lavish parties in pre-war America in the 20s and 30s. Even though she was born in 1859 in New York and died in 1950 in Versailles, France, this phrase beautifully describes what I learned from our Southern culture growing up:

Be pretty if you can
Be witty if you must,
But be gracious if it kills you.
—Elsie de Wolfe

I believe that most good people do the very best they can under the circumstances in which they find themselves. Some are able to go forward to achieve their hopes and dreams with the help of a Higher Power and are fortunate enough to have a few special people in their lives to inspire them. This has been so true for me beyond any expectations. You know who you are, and I want everybody else to know who you are too!

So, I say ahead of time to my old friends and my new ones: Bless Your Heart for joining me in the good and bad times! If you are not familiar with "Bless Your Heart," it is a truly handy little phrase. Mostly it is used in a caring way to refer to someone who is doing his or her best, such as a heartfelt, "She works so hard and goes home and takes care of all those children. Bless Her Heart." Sometimes, this time honored Southern phrase can dish out the negative masquerading as a positive, such as, "She just can't get to church on time no matter how hard she tries. Bless Her Heart." It can be either the language of the gossip or the prayer of the caring.

I hope this gives you some idea of how we Southern Women feel about ourselves and others. At the very least, you'll have a chance of knowing if you're being loved on or insulted just by the tone of the woman saying to you, "Bless Your Heart."

CHAPTER 2

How I Got My Name

I was born on June 25, 1939, in Atlanta Georgia, at Crawford W. Long Hospital. Crawford W. Long is an old Atlanta hospital dating back to 1908, opened by Dr. Edward Campbell Davis and a former student of his, Dr. Luther C. Fischer, as the Davis-Fischer Sanatorium on Crew Street near the present-day Turner Field. It had 26 beds. Dr. Fischer delivered all ten children born to my grandparents, Clifford and Mollie Barfield, and they named the sixth child Luther Fischer Barfield, after Dr. Fischer. In 1931, the hospital was renamed Crawford W. Long Memorial in honor of the Georgia physician who discovered ether as an anesthetic and was the first to use anesthesia during surgery.

The hospital quickly outgrew its capacity, and Davis and Fischer moved the hospital to its present site on Linden Avenue in 1911, expanding to 85 beds. Today, it is known as Emory University Hospital Midtown, with a total of 511 beds, but Emory committed to honor the original name, and the main façade has been preserved in its 1911 state.

LYNNE, ONE YEAR OLD, ATLANTA, JUNE 10, 1940

It was a year before the beginning of World War I. My parents, Dorothy and A D Barfield, were expecting a boy. In those days, there was no way to determine the sex of an expected baby. Surprised with a girl, Mama suggested "Why don't we name her Eddie since it sounds like A D?" Daddy was named after his Grandfather, and while it was true that the A and D had no periods after them, the family used to tease him and say, "Your *real* name is Abraham Darlington!" These were fighting words. My Aunt Irene, Mama's sister and best friend, suggested, "That's a cute idea to name her Eddie, but what do y'all think about Lynne for her middle name?"

Most Southern girls at the time had a double name, such as Mary Jane, Linda Sue, or Rebecca Ann, and were called by that double name. For the boys, there were quite a few "juniors" and the unfortunate ones who were a "III," which was pronounced "The Third" but ended up being nicknamed "the Turd!"

Because Lynne is a good "filler name" like Ann, and because they love me, 13 mamas have named their babies after me, using Lynne as a middle name.

CHAPTER 3

A Big Loving Family

The family home was on Mason Avenue in downtown Atlanta and is now long gone. Despite my research, I can't find out what the street name is now. Uncle Honey told me later that "the house was very large with many bedrooms," but I don't remember going further than the living room, dining room, and kitchen.

I never knew a lot about my grandfather, Clifford C. Barfield, other than he was killed in a Model T Ford auto accident at age 54 on June 22, 1924. The family story goes that it happened at an intersection. I didn't know until very recently that my Uncle Hinton, was in the car with my grandfather. He told his son Raymond that he always felt guilty because he felt he should have been driving. Incidentally, many of the Barfield men were not good drivers. One of Hinton's brothers, my Uncle Tinley (Tim), was involved in an automobile accident when he was an older man in his eighties, and the police came to check it out. When he was telling the story later, a relative asked, "Tim, did the police come?" and Uncle Tim said, "I don't know. I didn't have my glasses on."

CLIFFORD AND MOLLIE BARFIELD

My grandfather's death left my grandmother, Big Mama, to raise her ten kids and also take in some of her children's babies as well. It must have been hard for Big Mama to raise the children by herself.

Big Mama always looked very old to me. She was a large woman with rimless glasses and wore her hair pulled back in a bun. She wore soft voile dresses with lacy collars, and she always smelled so good, a fragrance which I later learned was lavender. She had plush, full breasts that were great for hugging. I could get my whole head in between her breasts when she hugged me!

She was greatly loved by her children and grandchildren. She had a wonderful smelling drawer—lavender again—and it was full of colorful ribbons that she allowed me and the cousins to play with. She always took sides with the grandchildren when a behavior problem came up. All of us grandchildren were fond of whispering in her ear something that might possibly get our parents in trouble. I remember telling her that I was hungry, and she said, "A D, don't you ever feed this precious little girl?" Not long before she died, I remember that all of her kids celebrated her birthday and pitched in and bought her a large mirror for the living room. She was *so* proud of it. I wonder what happened to it.

I was young, but I remember the smells coming from the small kitchen on Sundays when she had the whole family over. It's interesting that I remember the kitchen as small because most children remember things as being big. She did have a big black pot in her back yard where she either washed clothes, cooked, or maybe both. After a full Sunday dinner, the men would sit on the front porch and rock while the women removed their girdles and cleaned up. My cousins and I would play underneath the latticed porch where the old folks were rocking, not minding the weeds that tickled our legs.

I have a picture of Big Mama with her ten children. She is seated in the middle of them all with one of those fur skins around her neck, the kind where the animals are looking with their beady little black eyes and have their mouths open to attach to the tail of another. The children are all grown in the picture and Big Mama is no longer "Big." She is a tiny little old Southern lady who is ready for a rest from her labors.

TOP ROW (L-R): *UNIDENTIFIED, PROBABLY FRIEND OF THE FAMILY; LUTHER BARFIELD; HINTON BARFIELD; LUCILLE BARFIELD; ELIZABETH BARFIELD; TINLEY BARFIELD; SAM KING.* MIDDLE ROW: *"BIG DADDY" CLIFFORD C. BARFIELD; "BIG MAMA" MARY MOLLIE EASON BARFIELD, HOLDING BABY CAROLYN KING; GLORIA BARFIELD, WIFE OF HINTON; ANNIE CLIFFORD BARFIELD KING, HOLDING BABY RAY KING, CAROLYN'S TWIN BROTHER.* BOTTOM ROW: *JACK KING, SON OF SAM AND CLIFFORD; HOWARD BARFIELD; CARROLL C. BARFIELD A.K.A. HONEY.* NOT PICTURED: *A D BARFIELD AND HARRY BARFIELD.*

CHAPTER 4

Ancestry

As far as ancestry goes, we know that Daddy's mother's name was Mary Miriam Eason, known as Mollie to all of her friends and family. She died at the age of 69; I was six years old. At the funeral, one of the relatives asked Daddy, "Are you going to let Lindy kiss her goodbye?" Daddy was horrified and said, "No, I don't want her to feel that Mama is cold." I really think Daddy wanted to distance himself from the casket and his mother. People have their own ways at a funeral.

Mollie's family came to America from England through Savannah with General Oglethorpe and settled in Claxton, Georgia, about 50 miles from Savannah. Claxton is world famous for delicious fruit cakes—yes, a delicious fruit cake really does exist! It has always been a family joke that "fruit cakes" fit our family very well.

When I was about eight, the whole family went to an Eason family reunion in Claxton. Unfortunately, my cousins and I did not fully appreciate the historic occasion. Bobbie, Billie and I were too busy laughing and acting silly to pay attention to our rich history. We got dirty looks from our parents and plenty of shushing, but there was strength in numbers, and we ignored them. All that I remember hearing is that General Oglethorpe was onboard, and there were "preachers" in the family who were also on the boat from England which brought our ancestors to Savannah, their port into the New World. This particularly pains me now as later I earned my Master's in Historic Preservation, which became my interest late in life, and no one in the family kept any notes on the occasion.

CARROLL C. BARFIELD,   A D BARFIELD

A.K.A. HONEY, AGE 17

Daddy's Father was of Irish descent, and the Barfield family resemblance was strong in all of the children with their dark wavy hair. Daddy and Honey were two of 7 boys and 3 girls. My own two boys, Dixon and David, would inherit the dark wavy hair. They both look like Barfields to me, although the youngest, David, has a lot of his own father's features. Unfortunately, there was a vicious alcohol gene which ran rampant among the Barfield men. This led to an untimely death for some and problems in marriage for others, my parents among them.

My mother's mother was Bessie Moore, and her father was Stanford Still Lacy. The family originated in Helena, Arkansas, but I don't know any ancestral history. My mother's father died young, and her mother remarried a man named Joe E. McDonald, known to all as Daddy Mac. Bessie died at age thirty-five in childbirth with her eighth baby. With Grandfather Lacy, my grandmother had Aunt Irene, Dorothy (my mother), Aunt Evelyn, and Uncle Stan. With Daddy Mac, she had my Uncle Joe, Uncle Dave and Aunt Beth. After Daddy Mac died, the children were parceled off to different members of the family, but they managed to always remain close to one another, even in adulthood and marriage, and they saw to it that I got to see my cousins Nancy and Melinda, Sadie Ann, Bettie Lou, and Little Stan at family reunions every now and then.

LYNNE AND AUNT IRENE BEASLEY, AROUND 1941

My mother and her sister Irene were given to their Aunt Mamie, who had a daughter of her own and, of course, was partial to her and not happy about having to take Mama and Irene. Whether or not this contributed to Mama's personality problems in later life, I don't know. Irene lost her husband at age 42 and then got a nursing degree and supported her two children until they were grown. Irene was kind of the back bone of the family, keeping all of them in touch and organizing to get them together at Christmas and holidays.

(L-R), **Aunt Agnes Nabers, Mama (Dorothy), Aunt Mamie, Aunt Irene on Easter Sunday, April 1941**

CHAPTER 5

My Parents' Marriage: An Unlikely Romance

*B*efore the war and before they were married, Daddy had played the trumpet with Tommy Dorsey and Benny Goodman as an older teenager during the Depression. I have the pictures to prove it! Everyone in the family said, "A D just picked up the trumpet one day and started playing it." He went on the road with these bands before the war and had some funny stories about stopping in little towns. He told us about the different accents he heard from place to place.

I'm not sure how my parents met, but I had been told that Mama was a singer in a band. There is no one left who really knows. I treasure photos of Daddy playing with Tommy Dorsey in the basement of the old Roxy Theater in Atlanta. Also in the picture is Albert Coleman, who directed the Atlanta Symphony for many years. When my father died, my brother and I thought about burying his Olds trumpet with him. We

DOROTHY, A D, AND BABY LYNNE, JULY 1939

also entertained the idea of having a New Orleans Funeral, complete with walking under umbrellas. I'm so glad we didn't. Later, Larry's boy, Trace, would exhibit the same God-given talent that Daddy had, and he now plays the antique Olds trumpet that Daddy left to my brother.

The bands that Daddy played with were on the road quite a bit. During the Depression, the musicians in the band were all members of the Musicians Union, and they had contracts to play at hotels and parties. During the height of the Depression, Daddy recalled that they were booked into a prominent hotel in Chicago, but nobody could afford to come and dance, so the band played for four hours to an empty room to fulfill their contract and get paid!

TOMMY DORSEY, DADDY, ALBERT COLEMAN, UNKNOWN TRUMPETER, AND
RAMONA DAVIES, REHEARSING IN THE ROXY THEATRE, DOWNTOWN ATLANTA

During this period, Daddy was the only one working in a house full of children, most of whom were grown, married and had moved back home to Big Mama's with their own children. This had to be a very hard time for all of them after my grandfather was killed. Big Mama advised her children never to marry. She said "Marriage is just too hard!" As a result of this, every last one of the kids just ran off and got married, and she never witnessed any of their weddings.

My Mama and Daddy were both good-looking people. My Mother, Dorothy, had blond hair and was very beautiful with very light blue eyes, the kind that are almost see through.

There was never a doubt that they were in love. They shared the passionate kind that sometimes makes other people invisible to them, which included my brother and me. Their whole marriage was plagued by bouts of drinking and fighting, then holing up in the bedroom, sometimes not even coming out for a meal. According to the sounds we heard, we supposed they were making love or sometimes fighting. Daddy was not consistent in the way he treated her.

DOROTHY LACY BARFIELD

Jealousy combined with alcohol made fighting a constant presence in our house. He would buy her fashionable clothes and hats and insist that she draw her lipstick way over her natural lip line. All of my cousins remember this about her. He liked to show her off, but then would turn around and beat her so badly that she couldn't leave the house until the bruises had faded. For some reason—I remember this so well—he didn't like for her to sing in the car, although she was a good singer. Both of them were jealous and suspicious of the other.

It was interesting to me that the only time there was peace and no drinking in the house was when they were really mad at each other. I was always happy when they were mad at each other. However, when it came to decisions, whatever my father wanted was all right with her. Even later when he got custody of both of us in the divorce, it was all right with her. This was in the late forties and early fifties, and at that time, it wasn't easy to take children away from their mother and for a father to get full custody, but my father had considerable influence with lawyers and judges in Atlanta, most of whom were fellow Masons and Shriners. On reflection now, she could not have taken care of us on her own.

Just like she was with men, Mama was admired by other women. At one point in the forties, she had a cotton dress that was missing several buttons, which started at the neck and went all the way down the front. It was wartime, and buying matching buttons was not an option. She took the mismatched buttons from her button box and sewed them on her dress. Soon, the neighborhood ladies were doing the same thing; copying someone is one of the highest compliments, I think. She was naturally friendly, loved family, and got along well with the neighbors. I didn't know until many years later that her blond hair was not naturally blond. It was just that my father wanted her to be a blond. She actually had dark hair like mine.

CHAPTER 6

Pearl Harbor

Daddy told me that I was standing up in the front seat of our car on December 7, 1941. We were waiting on a light to change at the intersection of two streets in our neighborhood when he heard the shocking news on the car radio that the Japanese had bombed Pearl Harbor. I would have only been two and a half years old, but I do remember standing up in the front seat and how upset Daddy was, talking out loud to no one in particular about the horror of the news.

The impact of this was that Daddy and my Uncle Honey, who were pilots, were called in by the Army to train "six-week wonder pilots." This was a hurry-up plan to get the new pilots in the air to help fight the war, including training the student pilots to take off from a battleship and then land again.

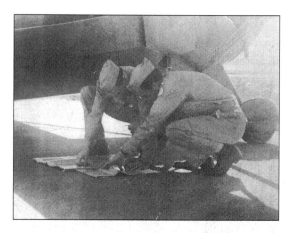

DADDY AND UNCLE HONEY AT MARSHALL FIELD, MIAMI, FLORIDA

DADDY (3RD FROM LEFT), HONEY (4TH FROM LEFT)

CHAPTER 7

The 40s

It is 1941 or 1942. I'm a toddler, probably about two and a half or three. It is a very hot night in Miami, Florida at the Marshall Field Army Air Base. My Uncle Honey and my father were temporarily stationed at this air base to train the new pilots. They had been allowed to take their wives and children; they both had one daughter at that time. Uncle Honey and his wife had a little girl a year younger than I, named Bobbie, who became one of my very best friends for life. We are more like sisters.

The Army recruits would paint a battleship outline on the tarmac to simulate the dimensions of an aircraft carrier. Daddy and Honey had to teach the boys to "touch and go." This was not personally remembered by me, but Daddy and Honey would tell stories later about their experience and say that "some of the boys would just freeze in the air." One story Daddy told was how one young pilot-to-be "walked right through a propeller which was going so fast that he didn't see it." Of course, he died instantly.

DADDY'S ARMY AIR CORPS I.D. CARD

Memories of these days are very vague, as Bobbie and I were very young. I do have three vivid memories of that time. The first one is at night, and I'm supposed to be asleep on the top bunk of a bunk bed in a small room, located in the Army barracks where we were living. I can hear Daddy and Mama arguing, but I can't understand anything they are saying except that they are talking loud, and I can tell they are mad. What I see is fuzzy, but the kitchen door is cracked and I can see into the kitchen where they are. Their voices make me feel afraid, and they are pushing each other around. Somehow it is important for me, small as I am, to make them stop. There is no one else there to stop them. I climb down from the top bunk, partly holding and partly falling onto the wooden railings, and run into the kitchen crying, "No, no, no!" This was my very first memory of the beginning of trouble between them which would last as long as the marriage. This was also most likely the beginning of my feeling responsible for them.

LYNNE ON THE STEPS AT THE AIR BASE IN FLORIDA, AROUND 1942

Another memory of that time at the air base, is Mama carrying a trash can from the house to the big community garbage container outside. A huge black scorpion is sitting on top of the trash can, and I am walking behind Mama, who is holding a flashlight so that it is shining in the scorpion's eyes. "Lindy," she said, "if you shine a flashlight in their eyes, they can't see you, and they won't move or hurt you."

We soon moved on, to another air base where I remember large black and white tiles on the kitchen floor. There was a heat register in the middle of the floor in the kitchen with a large waffle-shaped vent. I was on one side of the room, and Mama is holding her hands out to catch me when I arrive on the other side. Toddling towards her, I fall, and both my hands land on the register, burning them. "Lindy!" she cried. This memory is probably because it was hot and burned my small hands. My memories of those days are hazy and skimpy.

CHAPTER 8

After the War

After the war, we moved in with my Aunt Elizabeth (Betsy) and Uncle Johnson, Sr., who had this wonderful old house with a sleeping porch, in College Park, a neighborhood in South Atlanta. Sleeping porches were prevalent in houses during the early19th century in the South. The houses were generally built to be self-cooling in the summer by the way they were facing, but it would take a while, so people would sometimes sleep on the sleeping porch instead of inside the hot house in the summer. The porch was screened in on two or three sides of a house, the sides most likely to catch a cool breeze.

The bedroom windows were very tall, and my cousin Carol and I could step through them to play on the sleeping porch. We played and were able to move our toys and playhouse boxes all over the sleeping porch.

COUSINS CAROL COLLINS, 7, AND LYNNE, 6,

AT AUNT BETSY'S HOUSE ON EASTER SUNDAY, 1945

Cousin Carol was a year older than I and was a great play-mate. We have remained good friends, and we participate in a Cousins' Lunch whenever we can. We also send each other $1 on our birthdays!

We were never bored, playing in the huge backyard which backed up to the house of Carol's Aunt Ida. Aunt Ida made wonderful cookies and other goodies, the best of which I remember being the sugared orange rinds. We ran in and out of her Aunt's house freely, and there was always some treat ready for us two little girls.

While we lived with them, which I think was just a summer, Mama was an excellent seamstress and made Carol and me matching outfits, including purses! Mama would put extra pleats, tucks and smocking here and there, and Carol and I were so proud to wear our clothes, thinking we were so adorable. One of my treasured pictures is of the two of us in Mama-made Easter dresses, which were a deep rose color. Carol and I would twirl around and pose for the adults in the house.

Aunt Betsy was the organist at her Christian church (Disciples of Christ) on the corner, which was very near the house. She would ask us, "Would you girls like to help me set up the communion for Sunday?" So Carol and I got to carefully pour the grape juice into the tiny glass cups for the next church service. We understood the importance of getting the communion service just right. "I couldn't do all of this myself," Aunt Betsy would say, making us feel so grown up and necessary.

Mama and Aunt Betsy became close friends while we were there. The two would cook together in the huge white kitchen, which had a large table in the center with lots of cabinets around the walls, and a screened door leading to the back yard which banged shut noisily whenever Carol and I ran through it, chasing each other and playing. "Girls, don't let the door bang shut!" we heard either from Mama or Aunt Betsy just about every time.

When we misbehaved, Aunt Betsy, who was kind but at the same time a no-nonsense Mom, would dish out the consequence to Carol, but Mama was never the one to discipline me. I would just get the "Just-*wait*-until your-Daddy-comes-home-and-hears-what-you-have-done" speech. That was

Daddy's job. Early on I realized that being good was better than misbehaving and getting one of Daddy's spankings. He used his hand or a switch, and he could hit pretty hard. I learned that being good served me well, and it still does.

COUSINS LYNNE AND BOBBIE

CHAPTER 9

Uncle Honey and Aunt Bee

My father's father was killed in a car accident when my Uncle Carroll, the youngest, was an infant. Uncle Carroll was "the seventh son of a seventh son," which he said gave him special insight and powers, such as being able to remove warts by rubbing them with a river rock. This was true! He did this for many people. Honey said, "Just send the person with the wart to a creek and let them choose a rock from the creek." Then he would rub their wart with the rock and a few days later it was gone!

Uncle Carroll's nickname, "Honey," was given to him by his lovely wife Ray. So, he was "Uncle Honey" to a lot of the family, especially the kids. In fact, his daughters always called him that, so that's the name I knew him by.

Honey and Ray were such a close couple that through the years, she automatically became "Bee" which went with "Honey." I'd say that their daughters started this as they were growing up, but I also wonder if Bee started it herself when she signed birthday cards with "Bee and Honey."

BEE AND HONEY, SUNDAY SCHOOL HALLOWEEN PARTY,

SANDY SPRINGS METHODIST CHURCH, 1972

What we all know is they lived a great love story. They met in Sunday School when she was sitting in front of him. The first time he saw her there, he pulled her chair back toward him and whispered in her ear, "You are the girl I am going to marry." At that time, she was 13 years old and he was 16. She looked just like the popular Victorian prints "Cupid Asleep and Awake." In her youth and into her old age, she had a beautiful angelic face. She had always told her two girls, Bobbie and Billie, that she was 14 and he was 17, but they found some old love letters later that told them differently. She finished high school before they told the family that they were married. She was 17, and he was 20. They were married for 77 years when Honey died.

Theirs was a true romance in every sense of the word. They had their squabbles and their own strong opinions, but when people would ask them "What is your secret to such a long, happy marriage?" they would always say passionately and loudly, "*Church!*"

I once asked Aunt Ray, "Who else did you date before Honey?" With a startled look, she answered, "Oh, Lindy, there was never anyone before Honey!"

Uncle Honey was the only one of the seven brothers who never, ever touched a drop of alcohol of any kind. He had watched his brothers get into big trouble with their drinking, and he said that he couldn't take a chance. He was afraid that if he took even one drink—even a glass of wine—he would become an alcoholic, a genetic curse which plagued many of the brothers. In older age he was a mentor and advisor to his children, nieces, nephews, and friends, including me. He was also a member of Mensa, the high I.Q. Society. He seemed to know a little bit about almost everything!

Uncle Honey was someone I could always go to for advice. So could anyone else. We could always count on him to tell the truth whether we liked it or not. He loved his wife and daughters, and all of his nieces and nephews, and he loved his church and was active in it all of his life.

The only time that I didn't take his advice was in 1975. I went over to talk to him and get his advice—and hopefully, his approval—about getting a divorce from my alcoholic husband of eighteen years. I was at the end of my rope. Although he was familiar with what was happening in my marriage, he frowned and said, "Lindy, you can't get a divorce." This was because divorce in his generation was frowned upon, and women were expected to put up with almost anything to avoid the smudge on the family name. To his advice, I replied, "Oh, yes I can." And I did. Except for this one time, he was a model to me as a father, and I and all of his nieces and nephews loved him dearly. Aside from family, Honey helped older friends with their bookkeeping and financial problems, and in later life he trained his daughter Billie to take his place.

UNCLE HONEY AND AUNT BEE, 77ᵀᴴ WEDDING ANNIVERSARY,
BRIGHTON GARDENS, DUNWOODY, 2011

Honey and Bee moved into an Assisted Living home in Dunwoody, Georgia. Honey lived to the age of 97. Although diminished by Alzheimer's, he would look forward to his beloved Ray coming to see him daily in the Alzheimer's unit. When he became unable to speak, he would take her arm and kiss it up and down.

CHAPTER 10

Growing Up in Virginia Highlands

M y cousins Bobbie and Billie and their family moved to Atlanta's West End, which was on the other side of town, but we all stayed close. We were in our first house in the Virginia Highlands neighborhood until I entered fifth grade and my brother Larry, who was four years younger, entered kindergarten at Morningside School.

The house had two tiny bedrooms, one bath, and a detached, one-car garage. It had a fireplace in the small living room and hardwood floors. Our house had a small screened porch to the side of the house, and in the backyard there was a picnic house with benches and an outdoor barbeque grill. Daddy paid $13,000 for the house with help from the Army. My brother and I had twin beds and shared a room which had one small closet and one chest-of-drawers. I still wonder how we got all of our clothes in that small closet and one chest-of-drawers. There was no air conditioning in the house. The windows were raised in the summer, and there were screens in all of them. I don't remember any fans, but surely there were some. It is interesting to see what young couples today feel would be their minimum requirements for a house.

BROTHER LARRY BARFIELD

The house was #862 on Kings Court, a "U" shaped street which could be entered in two different places from Amsterdam Avenue. It had sidewalks and plenty of trees and playmates, all of whom went to Morningside School. It was a true neighborhood of that time where everyone knew each other and doors were left unlocked in case you needed to go and borrow some sugar. The neighbor didn't even have to be at home.

There was a big bulldog that lived on the upper end of the "U." He was probably sweet, but I was afraid of him because he was really big and had an ugly face. I could see his teeth outside his lips with his under bite. He slobbered all the time. A lot. I rode the bus home from school, and I would get off and walk an extra block to the lower end of the "U" to avoid the bulldog. The dog would wait patiently for the kids to come home after school, and he seemed to know exactly what time it was.

There were sidewalk cracks, and we all thought if we stepped on a crack we would break our mother's back. The aging sidewalks were full of cracks, and it took some fancy footwork to avoid them. If it rained, there were also a lot of big juicy earthworms that crawled out on the sidewalks and slowed me down because I had to carefully step over all of them so they wouldn't be squashed.

My #1 fear is spiders, the second being large roaches. The furnace was in the dirt basement area, and I remember standing over the vent in the upstairs hall, feeling the wonderful warm air come up through the floor blowing into my bathrobe. That particular joy went by the wayside when I was standing there one night and a fat, black roach fell out of my bathrobe, causing a fear of roaches for the rest of my life. From then on when I kill one, I use almost a whole can of bug spray. My husband says that I am drowning them. They look like they are in their own little tiny swimming pool. Then I can't bear to clean them up. When I get the nerve to sweep them into a dust pan, I race to the toilet to flush them, hoping they won't come back to life.

The children in the neighborhood and connecting streets spent a lot of time skating and playing games. At the time, the skates fit on our own shoes and required a skate key to tighten them. I have such fond memories of the skate key that later as an adult I ordered one online and had it silver-plated to wear as a necklace. One night at choir rehearsal, my friend Cindy asked, "Lynne, Why do you have a skate key around your neck?" Another friend thought it was some kind of new Celtic cross!

We also played hopscotch. My favorite was, "Movie Star Hopscotch," which took at least two people to play. We would draw a diagram of blank boxes on the driveway with a piece of chalk with a box at the end to turn around so you could hop back. Each player would hop on one foot, alternating with her playmate and choose a block to put a movie star's initials on it with chalk, such as R.H. for Rock Hudson, or D.D. for Doris Day. Pretty soon all of the blocks would be full with initials, and we had to remember all of them. If a player couldn't remember one, she had to hop over the block. The first one to get to the end by remembering all of them won.

Other favorite games were Crack the Whip, Mother, May I?, and catching lighting bugs and putting them in a jar with holes in the cap. We also played Red Rover. These were girl games. The boys played jacks with a small ball and jack pieces, or Kick the Can. The boys also loved to play marbles. They would lean back on the heel of their shoe and spin around until they created a depression in the ground, into which they shot marbles to win.

Girls also played jump rope for hours on end—even my husband Noah confessed when he was about 12 years old that he liked playing jump rope with the girls. I wish I could remember more of our jump rope songs because they are disappearing from our culture, which hurts my preservationist self. Players could jump rope all by themselves, but usually two girls swung a big heavy rope and another girl would run into the middle to start jumping. One of our songs was:

Teddy bear, teddy bear	Teddy bear, teddy bear
Say your prayers	Turn off the light
Teddy bear, teddy bear	Teddy bear, teddy bear
Walk up the stairs	Say goodnight!

There was a deep ravine with a creek on our street, and huge old trees that required daredevil feats such as shimmying out on long branches to get over the creek. We would also swing from a rope over this creek, which was filled with tiny crawfish which we would catch. The kids would divide up into what I would call "good gangs" and name themselves after the streets. Our gang didn't have a name, but I remember one close by was "The Bellevue Battle Axes," named after Bellevue Avenue, and another was the "McLynn Monsters" after a street named McLynn. These "good gangs" were co-ed with a natural competition between the boys and girls. All of the kids we knew were very physically active. My friends Janice Townley, Nancy McMains, and I would ride our bicycles for miles to go to movies on a Saturday.

The Saturday movies were sacred to us. Most of us got 25 cents a week for our allowance. We would ride our bikes to either the Highland Theater or the Plaza Theater, which is still going strong today. Each of our 25 cents was spent on 10 cents for the movie with 2 cents tax. That left us with 13 cents, which could be spent on a coke for 5 cents, and a choice of favorite candy bar, another 5 cents which still left 3 cents. We all had favorite candy bars. Mine was either M&Ms or Necco Wafers.

The movie started at 10:00 a.m. with a serial, which was either a science fiction picture featuring Buster Crabbe and a flying saucer that twirled around with a string we could see, or a cowboy flick with Hopalong Cassidy or Bob Steele. The serial was an important part of the movie and would always end with someone in grave danger, like hanging over a cliff, being boiled in oil, or something designed to bring us back the next Saturday, for sure. After the serial came the "News of the Day" in black and white, usually news about the War and the troops. The movie was usually an early Technicolor movie like a romance featuring Doris Day and Rock Hudson or a musical like *Singing in the Rain*. There were no explicit sex scenes. God forbid! The couple might possibly share a chaste kiss and then the camera would pan up to the beautiful sky or down to a lovely ocean, leaving us to imagine what the heck they did next.

Janice and I went to the Plaza Theatre where the price of admission was cheaper if for those under twelve years old. Every single time we went, the old guy who took our tickets said, "I know you are over twelve!" He thought that because I was already 5'4" when I was in the 5th grade, taller than any of the boys. This man gave me so much grief that I got my mother to find my birth certificate, and I presented it to him at the movies. No trouble after that. Incidentally, I never got any taller.

JANICE TOWNLEY (TOP); LYNNE BARFIELD, AND NANCY McMAINS (BOTTOM) WITH JOY THE CAT, 1952

TV was in its infancy at this time, about 1945-1950. Thanks to a Shriners' raffle that my father won, we were the first on our street to have a television. The TV was black and white, and the screen was a teeny square in the middle of a gargantuan cabinet. Until 4 pm every day, there was nothing on but a test pattern featuring an Indian Chief and some other lines and squiggles. The kids in the neighborhood would come over at four, and we would watch Bob Steele, a cowboy with a big white hat. All of the good cowboys had a white hat, while the bad cowboys had black ones, so it was easy to keep up with the good guys and the bad guys. Sometimes we would all just sit and stare at the test pattern on the TV and swear that we saw some colors. At the end of the programming for the day, usually about 10:00 pm, they would show an American Flag and play the National Anthem. After that, it was shut-down time with the familiar test pattern until 4 the next day.

Radio also was a very big deal during this time, and I remember the whole family sitting and staring at the radio and listening to programs like *The Green Hornet, Lorenzo Jones and His Wife Belle*, and *Let's Pretend*, which was my favorite Saturday morning fairy tale program. I have always thought that reading books and using our imaginations can cook up better pictures than any movie or television show.

All of the mothers on Kings Court at that time were stay-at-home mothers. Mothers who worked were a rare exception, and there was usually only one car in the family, which the father drove to work and back. The mothers cooked, kept house, and welcomed each other into their homes, although things were not quite that way at my house. Of my own mother's cooking, I remember her making white divinity candy occasionally, which was delicious. She also would make spinach with boiled sliced eggs on top. I had a doll that ate with us in her own high chair, and I fed her all of the things I didn't want. My father just hated that doll which made it even more fun for me.

LYNNE AND HER DOLL, DOLLY

I especially remember my good friend Mary Ann Fudger and our escapades pretending to be Nancy Drew and Judy Bolt, girl detectives. Mary Ann got to be Nancy, the chief girl detective, which was only fair as she was a couple years older than I. I was her sidekick detective, Judy Bolt. Mary Ann and I enjoyed acting out these stories that we read. Once, when we were on a dangerous assignment, we climbed into her father's car and pretended we were chasing some crooks. Mary Ann pumped the gas pedal, and I kept yelling, "Faster, faster! They are getting away!" This flooded the car engine, getting us into really big trouble with Mary Ann's father.

We also loved playing Telephone Operator, which back then meant plugging phone lines to connect people with their party. Naturally the home phones were rotary. With telephone service also being in its infancy, there was one phone in your house connected to the wall. It was sometimes shared with another family, which was called a "party line." Ideally it would ring maybe once for one family and twice for the other family, but sometimes they would pick up and listen to the other's conversation, and sometimes someone might quietly pick up and listen to theirs! Anyway, to connect calls, operators in a building miles away would use little connection wires and plug them into a giant bank of holes. So, Mary Ann and I hammered nails into the side wall of our little one car garage and tied strings on them so that we could "make calls" and "connect people with their friends!" I got a big spanking for that great idea.

Despite the idyllic description of life at this time, my brother Larry and I did not have any "spend-the-night" playmates. We never knew when there would be a bad night with a fight between our parents. However, we did spend the night with our friends. The parents never questioned what our home life was like, but they all shared picking us up and taking us to parties and events at the church, so I'm sure they knew.

During the late 40s, my father did not go on the road with a band anymore, but he did have his own band, "Eddie Barfield and His Band." "Eddie" was a nickname for A D. They would play for celebrities who would come to Atlanta and do a show in the big movie houses in downtown Atlanta.

Daddy's band would play down in the orchestra pit during the acts. There were no large neighborhood movie houses to accommodate special events. Everybody had to go downtown to the large movie houses like The Paramount, The Roxy, The Loews Theater, and the Rialto. The Rialto is still in operation and is owned by Georgia State University. I just love it to pieces that they saved the Rialto!

Larry and I have vivid memories of a bizarre game that Mama and Daddy used to play with us when we lived on Kings Court. They told us that there was a creature that lived in our attic named "The Dutch Doll." Occasionally, The Dutch Doll would come to see my brother and me. We were terrified of this thing. Mama would slide under the bed with her legs and feet sticking up beside the bed, and then Daddy would put a sheet over them, draw a man's face with eyebrows and blue eyes, then add a necktie and top it off with a hat. We were allowed to ask The Dutch Doll questions, and Mama would make it answer "yes" or "no" by moving her feet up and down for "yes" or side to side for "no." Once Mama put fresh sheets on Larry's bed and The Dutch Doll's face had not completely washed off. He leaped out of bed saying "The Dutch Doll is in my bed!" and climbed in my bed that night! My research on The Dutch Doll has turned up nothing. If you find out anything about The Dutch Doll game, please let me know. I can't believe they thought this up by themselves.

BROTHER LARRY WITH COOKIE THE ESKIMO SPITZ

We had a darling Eskimo Spitz puppy named Cookie, who loved me and Larry, but no one else. I remember that we found her dead at the foot of Larry's bed one morning. Daddy said that probably someone in the neighborhood had poisoned her. This was the first loss of a dear pet for us.

The family car during this time had a running board, which was fun to sit on and eat a snack at one of the few drive-in restaurants available at the time. Since families only had one car, everyone walked, rode their bike, or caught a bus on Highland Avenue, about a half mile from our house. There was a grocery store on the corner of Highland Avenue and Amsterdam Avenue called Vrono's Grocery. Mama would give me a grocery list, which she usually wrote on the back of a family photograph, and I would walk up to Vrono's and get the items. Many of my old photographs from that time have grocery lists on them, such as "Bruton Scotch Snuff, 11 cents, Colgate tooth powder, 10 cents, and bar soap, 10 cents."

The grocery store had a floor made of old wood, a paddle fan on the ceiling, and big jars of candy on the counter. The store had a distinctive smell, which wasn't bad, it was just distinctive. Mr. Vrono was a butcher, and I could watch him cutting the meat behind the refrigerated counter with his bloody apron on. There were large glass bowls of penny candy. Even at my young age, I wasn't given any problem when buying Mama's cigarettes. At that time, I don't think they had figured out that smoking could kill you.

In back of Vrono's Grocery was the Charme Beauty Salon. I had a head full of thick black hair, which I wore long until after elementary school. My first permanent was using one of those huge old silver permanent machines with the electrical wires dropping down to a curler attached to your hair. It's a wonder that women didn't get electrocuted. That process usually dried the hair to a crisp, so the next step was to have a hot oil treatment to get it back in shape. I usually had a head full of oily, greasy hair, and one of my friend's mothers asked me not to lean back on her upholstered chair, which hurt my feelings at the time.

Delivery men were common in the 1940s. The iceman came to deliver a big block of ice, which he picked up with huge ice tongs. The ice was placed in the refrigerator to keep the food cool. We did get a modern refrigerator later while living in Virginia Highlands. The Highland Bakery man would come around to deliver bread and baked goods. He had a fabulous chocolate cake that I looked forward to. It wasn't unusual for my Aunt Irene to call us on a whim and announce that she had just bought a chocolate cake from the Highland Bakery man and say "Why don't we all go on a picnic?" The milkman, on a schedule that suited the family, delivered the milk. He just put the milk on the front steps, and we could see the cream on the top of it. The milk bottles were sealed with little round cardboard seals. The bottles were made of glass, and the name of the dairy was imprinted on the side. Larry and I loved to peel off the top seal and drink the cream. The birds also liked the cream, and if they beat us to it, they would peck through the seal. We also had deliveries and pick-ups from the dry cleaners. Ours was named Clark Laundry.

The kids played all day outside in the summer, and the mothers would drag us into the house just long enough to eat supper before we would go back outside again to play on the grass. I remember lying on my back in the grass with Mary Ann Fudger, staring up at the sky, holding my eyelids open so I wouldn't miss seeing a shooting star. I never actually saw one but never gave up hope.

As I write this, I am 76 and have only seen three real shooting stars in my life. Now, I have stars painted on our bedroom ceiling. The paint is fluorescent and gathers light during the day. I enjoy the night sky when we go to bed. It features three shooting stars, and the sky as it appeared on the night Noah and I married in 1979. We got the idea when we went to a home show at the Galleria Home Show about five years ago. There was an artist named Michael who had a trailer inside. After entering with all of the lights on, he instructed us to close our eyes for about 10 minutes and then open them. Amazingly, the ceiling on the trailer was full of stars! So we hired him to come to our house. He went into the bedroom and covered the windows with black plastic and announced that he would be coming out in four hours, which he did. Having told him that I had only seen three shooting stars, he painted three more on the sky just for me. We have enjoyed surprising our friends when they come over for the first time to see the night sky. It's easy to fall asleep looking at it. During the day it's a normal, everyday white ceiling; it will be a big surprise for whoever buys our house one day.

CHAPTER 11

Blackstone the Magician and His "Plant"

Blackstone the Magician came to the Loews Grand Theater once a year. At the time, he was as popular as Houdini. I was privileged to be a "plant" in the audience for him. I was probably 8 or 9, and I sat on the first row for the show. Daddy's band was in the orchestra pit.

Blackstone, dressed in all black with a black top hat, would ask "Is there was a little girl in the audience who would like to pull the rabbit out of the hat?" My job was to raise my hand high and shake it around wildly. Then he called me up to the stage and pulled a live fuzzy white rabbit out of the hat and gave it to me along with a box of chocolates!

A POSTER ADVERTISING BLACKSTONE THE MAGICIAN, C. 1947

After the show was over, I went backstage, and Daddy introduced me to the crew. I stood on top of an orange crate, holding the corners of my skirt out a la Shirley Temple, and said, "I'm a Georgia Peach!" They clapped and laughed, but probably didn't understand anything I said. Interestingly, Blackstone's stage crew was, I think, Romanian. In any case, they spoke no English, but smiled and nodded their heads.

I did this for at least three years and got three rabbits and three boxes of chocolates. Daddy built a rabbit hutch in the backyard for them, and yes, they multiplied. We gave a few of them away, but I don't remember what happened to all of them, only that the kids on the block enjoyed them.

The only other celebrity that I remember meeting was Hopalong Cassidy, a popular cowboy actor, and again this was when Daddy's band played for his appearance. I have no memories of the show.

CHAPTER 12

The Morningside Experience

A round 1945, we moved into the Morningside area to Cumberland Road next door to Morningside Elementary School. Our teachers were wonderful, dedicated career teachers, and my friend Janice can recall the name of every teacher from kindergarten on up. The teachers were all "lifers" and not a single one left Morningside while we were there.

There was no middle school then. We went to elementary school through the seventh grade and then went directly to the eighth grade in high school. Our school was red brick and had shiny floors, which the janitor kept buffed to a high shine. The cafeteria was downstairs. There was a large play yard with metal swings and a small "hut" on the campus where groups occasionally made crafts, jumped rope, or had Scout or Camp Fire Girl meetings. There was an upper play yard and a lower one. For a short time after we moved to the neighborhood when I first attended Morningside, there was a forest of trees where Haygood Methodist Church would later be built. I used to take my paints and easel down to the property where they would later build the church, and paint. Once, when I had painted for about an hour underneath a tree, suddenly a boy who had climbed the tree said something and scared me to death!

There was very little relocation of children from other states, and when we did get someone who transferred in, it was like getting someone from another planet. Morningside was one of the schools, along with Samuel Inman (at the time an elementary school) and Spring Street Elementary that fed into Grady High School. Most of us went all the way from kindergarten through seventh grade at Morningside and then on to Grady High School together. We were like brothers and sisters and still are. We still have a good crowd when we celebrate a reunion for Grady High School.

Neither my mother nor father were readers, except for Daddy who loved the newspaper. And I loved the newspaper too. Actually, I first learned the truth about Santa Claus at age 10 when I read "Ripley's Believe It or Not" in *The Atlanta Journal* that there was once a *real* Santa Claus! Talk about disappointed! It sounds crazy to be ten years old before I found out the truth about Santa, but that's so me. I desperately wanted Santa to be real and wouldn't give it up until I read it in the paper. At Morningside we had a large play yard and plenty of physical activities planned, including a yearly ferocious competition of running games and races between the two sides of "the blue" and "the tan."

The cafeteria was large, and students could buy hot lunches or bring lunch from home. We all had a lunch box with some popular character on it such as Hopalong Cassidy or Sky King. Mama always packed my lunch when I took it. Peanut butter and jelly sandwiches were the most popular lunch to come from home. Occasionally we would trade foods with other kids. Some things probably never change!

My most vivid memory was of boiled cabbage in our hot lunches. There wasn't a big choice in the "take it or leave it hot lunch." The cabbage was outstanding because they boiled it until it yelled for help and turned yellow. The smell of cabbage filled the school. Oddly enough, my friends Janice and Nancy don't remember the cabbage experience the same way I do, so I guess people remember different things. I like cooked cabbage now, but I don't overcook it.

We had a visit from Sky King at Morningside once. Sky was a cowboy who piloted an airplane! We did the usual field trips too, visiting the Mathis Dairy to see Rosebud the Cow, and going to the zoo as a class. Rosebud is still around, but is now a "pretend cow" made of sturdy plastic. She must have tired of kids trying to milk her. The zoo was not too great back when I was a little girl. I particularly remember Willie B., the huge Gorilla. Back then, Willie lived in a small room with a glass front where he would hurl himself against the glass in frustration. BOOM! In later years, Willie would enjoy a beautiful habitat much like his place of birth, and he even became a father at a late age. Zoo Atlanta is a wonderful place to visit where the animals have room to breathe, and it's easier for the people to breathe too. The Cyclorama was located directly next to the zoo while I was growing up. It is the largest Civil War painting in existence, housed in a round area. Currently, it is being moved to the Atlanta History Center, where it will be expanded to include never-before-seen pieces. Like the zoo, no doubt it will be something not to be missed when visiting Atlanta.

We always said the Pledge of Allegiance to the flag, and the day started with a prayer. No one questioned this—ever—and there was no outcry about praying. We learned to read from books with characters named Tom, Jerry, Spot, Dick, and Jane. What a pleasure it was to learn to read. When I'm in a flea market now as an adult, I look for these books, but they are beyond my ability to buy one. The copies I have found in my travels were over $300.00 each. What happened to all of them?

Janice, Nancy, and I collected trading cards with pictures on them, which we put in scrapbooks specifically made for the cards. None of us know what happened to our scrapbooks, and none of us have ever seen any in a flea market or antique store. The cards had different measures of value, just as baseball cards do. There was a pair with "pink girl" and "blue boy" and a pair with horse heads. We also collected key chains with various things on them, and we would attach them all together and wear them around our waists with the last one being a rabbit's foot. We were "cool" before "cool" was cool.

We rode our bicycles for miles and miles and miles. My bike was a light green Schwinn with purple striping and tassels hanging off the handlebars. I loved it dearly and wish I had it still. They were so easy to ride—pedal forward to go, pedal back to stop. No gears to worry about. We bicycled everywhere!

The Principal of Morningside Elementary was Mrs. Pounds. She was a very good and fair principal, and she stayed at Morningside for a long time just like the teachers. I was never called into her office for misbehaving, but my brother, Larry, was a different story! He would not take his papers home to be signed, and Mrs. Pounds was always calling my parents to complain, "Why can't Larry be a good student like his sister? Why won't he do his homework? He takes his papers and wads them up and stuffs them in his desk!" And so on…!

The kids in the class just above us were always highly respected by us. The boys in the seventh grade were allowed to be "patrol boys" and help the younger kids cross the street, but girls were not allowed to do patrol duty. We were also not allowed to wear pants of any kind to school, only dresses. Mrs. Pounds was very big on girls being little ladies. Good manners were expected and so was respect for our teachers. If we got into trouble at school or didn't do well with our studies, we could bet our parents would *not* be on our sides. It was the teachers and the parents together, a mighty force to reckon with. Throughout these schools years of 1945 to 1952, we received a terrific education from our dedicated teachers.

All of us loved going to school. It was popular to be good and to study and make good grades. Except for a few boys, most of us were very respectful and enjoyed all aspects of school. Of course we looked forward to the holidays and summer, but also looked forward to going back to school because that's where all of our friends were. Going back to school meant new sharpened pencils, a Blue Horse Notebook and blue lined paper, and usually new crayons.

Two incidences stand out vividly in my mind from Morningside — one was in the first grade. We had been working with wet clay in kindergarten, and my hands were all slippery. I asked if I could go to the bathroom and got permission, but my slippery hands couldn't open the door. I wet my pants in front of everybody and thought I would die from humiliation, but I didn't. I cried and Nicky Routsos pointed at me and said, "Lynne wet her pants!"

Another was we hung our coats, hats and gloves in little closets in the backs of our classrooms where the doors pulled down from top to bottom over them. It was such an honor to be asked to decorate the doors for different holidays and seasons all through elementary school. The more artistic students were usually picked to do this. Beating the erasers together to get rid of the chalk in them was another honor. We were encouraged to save aluminum foil and empty toothpaste tubes for the war effort, and some families had big balls of foil from saving a long time. Victory gardens were popular also, but our school didn't have one.

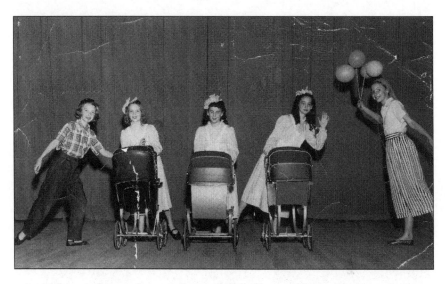

(L-R) Laura Smith, Louise Gregory McCahan, Nancy Thomas, Lynne
Barfield, and Suzanne Hemrick in *GiGi*, Morningside School, 7ᵀᴴ grade

One thing about elementary school troubled me then, and
as an adult, it still does. We had a very nice looking boy who
went to school with us, who was our age, but instead of going
to class, he sort of hung out with the school janitor. He wore
overalls and had bare feet, even in the wintertime. I never
saw him wear any shoes. He had two older sisters who had
attended Morningside before him, and they went on to high
school at Grady just like everyone else. I wondered then, and
still do, whatever happened to him. Why didn't one of the
teachers buy him some shoes? Why didn't our parents buy
him some shoes? What was wrong with this whole picture?
He did not seem in any way to be a "special needs" student.
I'd just like to know. I hope he is a successful, happy adult
with some nice shoes.

We looked forward to entering Grady High School with anticipation. We were quite immature when we entered high school at age thirteen. I remember my extreme disappointment when Valentine's Day came around because we didn't have a Valentine box like we did at Morningside. The seniors seemed almost like royalty since some of them were close to eighteen years old.

CHAPTER 13

Books, Ailments, and "Duck and Cover"

I fell in love with books very early. Learning to read was easy. The one and only time that my mother ever stood up to my father about anything was when we were living at 862 Kings Court in the Virginia Highlands house. She had ordered the whole set of *My Book House for Children* for me. It arrived one day in a big box. She had paid $25.00 for the whole set of thirteen books. Daddy told her, "Send them back immediately!" but she refused. She said, "Lindy loves to read, and I want her to have these books, and I won't send them back." I absolutely devoured those books and read all of them many times. My childhood was full of reading about Charles Kingsley's *Water Babies*, tales from Shakespeare, King Arthur and his court, and fairy tales of princesses letting their hair down from towers. The illustrations were awesome, delicate, and exquisite. It sure beat what was going on at my house; to lose myself in one of these books was to surround myself with an invisible wall.

My friends and I always read all summer with books from the library as well. We would receive a certificate for reading the books, a highly prized summer honor. Our library was at the corner of Highland Avenue and St. Charles Avenue. It is gone now. There is still nothing in its place, just a blank dirt square. My favorite story was *The Night Before Christmas*. I guess because it was the only one that Mama ever read to us. I still love it. She would prop up in bed with me and Larry and read it just right. I read it to my boys, the three of us propped up in bed, until they thought they were too old. I'm still not too old. Thank goodness.

At about age ten, returning a book one time, I had turned down a page of the book in order to save my place. The librarian, a mean-looking large woman with a head of bushy black hair, looked at me and said, "How would you like *your* arm bent behind your back?" Since that scary encounter, I have never turned down a page in a book for fear of somehow hurting it. I will use toilet tissue as a book mark if necessary before I will turn down a page in a book. There must be others out there like me, because sometimes I will buy a used paperback book and the last reader has gently turned down the very, very smallest corner, as though apologizing to the book ahead of time.

We did not have many vaccines available, so I and all of my friends had all the childhood illnesses. We had measles, mumps, and chicken pox, which we called "the chicken pops."

With measles, all of the windows had to be covered so that we didn't "ruin our eyes." I also remember having mumps at Halloween, and my friends came around to my bedroom window to sympathize. At the time, we didn't think about others catching it that way. There was no polio vaccine, and when I was little, especially in the 40s, it was a terrible worry for parents. A lot of public swimming pools were closed for fear of polio. There are adults my age today who still suffer the effects of having had polio before there was a vaccine. Some are having a recurrence of childhood polio.

We were required to have a small pox vaccination when we entered first grade. This was usually given on the arm, and many of the kids had to wear a plastic shield taped to their arms while the vaccination was "taking." My father didn't want me to have a scar on my arm, so he insisted that I be vaccinated on my thigh. When it was time for first grade I had to pull up my skirt so the nurse could look for the scar, but one was never found. This always resulted in the nurse calling Daddy to insist that "She *must* have proof of vaccination, Mr. Barfield!" However, Daddy would not allow it and swore that I had been vaccinated on my thigh, so we went through this scenario a couple of times with the nurse before she decided to forget the whole thing.

We also had dog tags in the early grades of Morningside. We said, "Look! We have our names and addresses on them just like the soldiers do, serving in the war!" They had a little notch in them to fit between our teeth. Little did we suspect that the tags were in case of a bombing, and the notch was in case we had a seizure, and the dog tag itself would prevent our swallowing our tongues and would the identification of our bodies.

This was toward the end of the World War II. And we practiced "Duck and Cover" under our desks, as if that would have really helped during a bombing. I don't remember any of us being anxious or thinking there was a real threat to us.

OUR VERY OWN DOG TAGS IN ELEMENTARY SCHOOL

DUCK AND COVER

CHAPTER 14

What is Normal? A Continuing Nightmare

School was my love and salvation from what was happening at home. My true life was at school. On the home front, things got worse. My mother sank further and further into alcoholism and depression, and so did my Dad, but he continued to go to work at the Harry Barfield Printing Company that he owned with my Uncle Honey. This made for some nights without supper for Larry and me. Larry and I tried to open a can of something with a hammer and a nail because Mama and Daddy had passed out one night and we were hungry.

Their fights got worse and worse. I suppose I can say to his credit that Daddy never laid a hand on me or my brother except for the occasional spanking that was deserved. Sometimes Mama would attempt to call the police, but Daddy would grab the phone and rip it completely out of the wall. The first time this happened, I was so shocked I felt numb. Once, I called the police myself before he could get to the phone. Two officers came and stood in front of all of us in their neat blue policeman uniforms and asked Mama, "Do you want to press charges, ma'am?" There she stood drunk and beaten, looking so small and defenseless, in front of the policemen. My father gave her a "look," and she bowed her head and said, "No." I watched the police car drive away, and I never called them again to come and help us. It was hopeless. I felt that no one cared, and no one could help us. Larry and I would cling together until these episodes were over. We had each other, but Mama did not have a hope in the world.

Another time, I had a loose baby tooth. It wasn't unusual for a parent to tie a string around a baby tooth and tie the string to the door and then slam the door. They really did. But with this loose baby tooth, Daddy was drunk and instead pulled a permanent tooth in my jaw area with pliers. It bled and bled on my pillow and scared me with all of the blood, which I couldn't get to stop. So I went into my parents' bedroom and could not wake up either one of them. I sat straddling Daddy's stomach, beating my fists on his chest to wake him and tell him about the blood, but it was impossible. I went back to my bedroom and cried myself to sleep.

About this same time when I was about 8 years old and we were still living in the Virginia Highlands House, Mama got pregnant. Nobody said anything to me about it. I did notice that her tummy was getting bigger, but didn't think much of it. One night they had one of their humdinger fights, and Daddy threw her against the stove. The next day she and Daddy left without saying where they were going. They got a sitter for us and came home two days later and told me that I had had a baby sister, but she only lived 6 hours and then died. They had named her Elizabeth after my Aunt Betsy. They had had a funeral and buried her in the family cemetery plot in College Park, Georgia. It was like a punch in the stomach for me. I had a sister and she died? She just hadn't been able to make it alive as a result of their last drunken fight. I think of her often and what it would have been like to have had a sister.

Our relatives were busy with their own lives, but Larry and I would occasionally get to stay with my Uncle Honey, Aunt Bee and their girls while Mama was sent to Milledgeville Hospital, for alcoholism. It was called The Georgia Lunatic Asylum in the beginning, then Central State Hospital, and lastly when Mama was there, Milledgeville Hospital. It was still using "backward methods," and involuntary sterilizations were being performed there. It was assumed that everything was Mama's fault. Larry and I were not told what was happening there.

The treatment for alcoholism in the 40s was electroconvulsive shock therapy. We would visit her at Milledgeville while she was being treated. At the time, the hospital at Milledgeville was a dumping ground for mental patients and patients considered to be a high risk to themselves or others. She wasn't allowed to have anything sharp such as a razor to shave her legs. She would come back home like a zombie; not herself, at least not drinking, but also not remembering much of anything. As she improved, Daddy would bring home the booze, and it would start all over again.

During this time in the late 40s, I concentrated on school, my grades, and friends. I loved learning with all of my heart and soul. I had a problem getting to sleep during this whole time, and I have pictures of myself with circles under my eyes. Never once did I feel as though Larry and I were the cause of any of my parents' problems. I understand now that it would have been typical if we had felt that way. However, I did feel responsible for them, which lasted until they both died. Daddy died on my 33rd birthday when he was 63, and Mama, then living in Florida, died when she was 57.

I was desperate for my parents to get a divorce. I didn't see how we could go on as a family. I had long hair which was slightly curly at that time. I wore it in long separate curls which I made by wrapping my hair around my finger with a comb. I made a deal with God during this time, and I promised Him that if he let my parents get a divorce, I would cut off my hair. Later, when they did get a divorce in 1952, I cut my hair to make good my part of the deal. Part of the divorce settlement was that she was never to get in touch with us or ever come back to Atlanta. And she didn't.

We had a string of housekeepers after Mama left us to live in Florida. Some of the housekeepers were very nice. My favorite one was actually named Pearl Ring. She loved me and taught me to crochet and cook a few things. She had weekends off and chose to take me with her to visit her daughter. She would talk about how smart I was learning to crochet and how I fixed my own hair. However, we had one housekeeper who climbed into bed with Daddy one night; he let her go immediately.

CHAPTER 15

Jarene Townfovska and Lene Barfilova, Future Ballerinas

We were very fortunate to have ballet lessons as well as music and theater throughout the whole seven years at Morningside. We always felt sorry for an incoming student who had not had this extra training. We had a wonderful teacher, Miss Hilda Gumm, who single-handedly cranked out recitals and pretty darn good plays. We used to have other schools visit Morningside just to see our productions. After leaving Morningside, Janice and I, as did our friends Annetta McConnell, Virginia Smith, and many of the other girls, went on with private ballet lessons.

Annetta McConnell Ohlendorf, Lynne
Barfield Byrd, Janice Townley Moore

Janice and I vowed that the two of us would never marry and that we would be ballerinas and live in a big house together with a bunch of cats. We would sacrifice marriage and children so we could devote ourselves to our art. We pretended to change our names to sound Russian. Janice Townley was "Jarene Townlovska" and I, Lynne Barfield, was "Lene Barfilova." It kept us very dreamy and imaginative, and I'm sure it kept us out of trouble. Some of our other girlfriends fell in love with horses, which kept them out of trouble too.

As an adult poet, Janice wrote a poem about us during this would-be ballerina time:

Ballet in the Fifties
by Janice Townley Moore

Cold war or not,
Russian names glided off our tongues:
Danilova, Pavlova, Toumanova.
Our fathers grimaced at our pink toe shoes,
Teased that hound dogs could point as well
We should be stenographers or nurses.
Still, we *bourreed* and *plied*,
Switching easily to the French
of the art we suffered for.
In letters to each other we dreamed,
"Ma petite, the lights are dimming.
We shall dance before the queen":
She, Lene Barfilova of Swan House,
And I, Jarene Townloska, of Ballet Nest,
Ignorant of Russian phrases.
"Years from now, *ma Cherie*,
They will gaze upon our well-worn slippers
En pointe under the polished bell jar."
Meanwhile, we saved our allowance,
Did a *grande jete* away from our fathers
Into balcony seats at the Fox.
We envied each ballerina in Communist tulle,
Applauded her finesse
Pirouetting from behind the Iron Curtain.

Grady High School not only put on plays—Gilbert and Sullivan were the most popular—they also put on some good half-time shows! Our band director was very creative. I had a ballet partner who danced with me during those football halftimes. My dancing partner pursued his career in ballet, later went to New York, danced with a major ballet company, married a ballerina, came back to Atlanta, and opened a ballet school with his wife. They had two children together.

I had taken ballet for years, but, as I have already said, my father was not one who praised you if you weren't any good. He told that being a dancer was not a good choice for a career. Daddy, having been in show business, did not encourage us at all and told us that we were not good enough to make any money as dancers. "Dancers like you two are a dime a dozen." It turns out that he was right, but it seems that this is the complete opposite of parents today, who praise every small thing their children do, possibly encouraging them at things they really aren't good at, and probably never will be. Janice's father, who had a thriving insurance business, told us that unless we went to college we would end up as cashiers at Woolworth's Dime Store. We knew we didn't want to do that. Actually, I wouldn't have made a good cashier either.

Camp Toccoa

I started attending the Camp Fire Girls camp early with my cousin, Bobbie, and later with Janice. Camp Toccoa was in North Georgia. The camp was designed for two-week visits, and there were themes planned for the stay. After two weeks, I would come home, and it would seem as though I had been gone a long, long time.

The camp was divided into age groups. My Cousin Bobbie and I started out in Omixi, the location name for the younger campers, and then graduated to Yoki. The girl counselors were all together up on the mountain in an area called Keona. Of course, Camp Toccoa was only for young ladies. There was a boys' camp across the lake, but no boys at Toccoa! We did yell at them from across the lake while we swam and earned our swimming badges, and our counselors fraternized with their counselors.

Lynne, 11, and Bobbie, 10, at Camp Toccoa

During the time we went to camp, Bobbie's little sister Billie wanted to go and see what was happening at Camp Toccoa. She stayed in the Blue Bird's Nest. This was for the very youngest little campers. Bobbie and I had strict instructions from my Aunt Bee to look after little Billie, and we did. Camp was full of fun, campfires, ghost stories, tricks on the counselors, such as short-sheeting their beds and putting small frogs in them. My favorite two week theme was "Christmas in July." We had a huge Christmas tree which we decorated in the main lodge where we met for meals. We had all of the trimmings of Christmas. We had a big fire in the lodge fireplace and sang Christmas songs. It was just so very cool to be celebrating Christmas in the summer!

Much later, my granddaughter Sarah went to Camp Toccoa and stayed in the same cabin that I was in 40 years earlier. By that time, Toccoa had a fancy swimming pool, a fancy cafeteria, and boys!

CHAPTER 17

Christmas

Christmas remains my favorite holiday, and it takes me longer and longer to decorate each year. Our main tree is old fashioned and loaded every year with some expensive ornaments, but mostly with those that the boys made in grammar school, those the boys and I made with Granny Patrick, and ornaments from Noah to me and from me to him. Also some were made by Noah's daughter, Debbie, who is a gifted jewelry designer. One of the reasons it takes such a long time to decorate is because most of the ornaments get a "Ohhhhh!" from me like one that Dixon made in first grade, one that Dave made in kindergarten, and our very first Christmas ornament from another couple with "Byrd" engraved on its shiny glass. I divide them all into different piles before starting to decorate. There are the Angels, the Bears, the Red Apples, the Hanging Crystals, the Peppermint Sticks, and a pile of specialty ornaments with "Lynne" or "Lynne and Noah" on them. Of course, there's the long string of cranberries, artificial most years, to wrap around the tree first, and last but not least, the set of 12 "Noah's Ark" ornaments. If I have enough energy after the tree is all finished, I throw some sparkle snow on it, and—ta dah!—the Christmas tree is done!

NOAH IS SANTA AT OUR HOUSE

My aim is that there can never be too many Christmas lights. That's just craziness, I know. In addition to our main tree, I have a cat tree, which is new to our Christmas decorations. My friends send me cards with pictures of cats, which I carefully cut out, punch a hole in the top, add a bow, and hang it on my cat tree by Halloween. I also add little artificial mice hanging by their tails, and of course, lights and a few ornaments. Halloween is my target date to start all of this decorating. Noah says our Christmas tree is the only one he has seen with dust on it. For the last five years I have thought to myself, "I won't do this next year," but I always do.

One year we decorated our tree and took a picture with us on either side looking up at the top. Then Noah photo-shopped Abbie on top of the tree as though she was an angel. And under the tree, we printed, "Don't worry Abbie, it's only for two weeks!"

OUR CHRISTMAS CARD WITH ABBIE ON TOP OF CHRISTMAS TREE, 2005

In the living room we usually have lighted Christmas houses and little people around them, singing or skating on a pond, which is really a mirror. We also have a nativity scene in the front yard with a spotlight on it, and luminaria along the front walkway.

ABBIE'S CHRISTMAS OUTFIT

Every Christmas, our church, Dunwoody United Methodist, asks us to submit a Christmas devotional, if we have one. Here's one I submitted of our Christmases with extended family:

Who is Your Family at Christmas?

Galatians 6:10, "So then, whenever we have an opportunity, let us work for the good of all, and especially for those of the family of faith."

Everyone who knows us well knows that Noah has had three wives, and they are dear to us and part of our extended family. When the first grandchild came, it made us realize that this little girl could have several grandmothers, not just two! Since some of our adult children are far away and can't always come home, our extended family spends holidays and birthdays together. Sometimes we add a couple of friends to the mix if they are alone for the holiday. We try to think of some special way to remember what Christ's birthday is all about.

About two years ago, we borrowed the costumes from the church after the live manger scene was over. As Noah read the gospel from Matthew with his melodious tenor voice, all of us had a part and a costume in acting out the birth of Christ. Noah's daughter was Herod. One ex-wife held the star, while her husband was a shepherd. Another former wife was an angel. Yes, we took some liberties with the story. We didn't have anyone to play Baby Jesus, so—I apologize, Lord—we put our toy poodle in a basket, and she was our Baby Jesus. We all did a pretty good job, and it was a special, very warm Christmas, maybe our favorite.

So the question is, "Who is Your Family?" Of course, it is your family and loved ones and maybe even the stranger that Jesus told us to ask. Our church, at Christmastime especially, makes me think of our members as family when we worship together, sing carols, and enjoy many special Christmas events.

Prayer: Heavenly Father, how fortunate we are to have our own families and to be part of the Dunwoody United Methodist Church family! Thank you for those who lead us, those who celebrate with us, those who mourn with us, those who share your love in all that they say and do. May our actions and deeds be worthy of your love. Amen.

CHAPTER 18

The Morningside Mothers

I stayed positive and hopeful as a young girl because of my friends, school, and the wonderful Morningside Mothers. In the late 40s, some of the mothers got a car of their own: Mrs. McConnell, Mrs. Townley, Mrs. McMains, Mrs. Roach, Mrs. Ison, and Mrs. Smith. There were five or six of them who would take us to dancing lessons, Camp Fire girls meetings, movies, church, anywhere. They were absolutely devoted to us. As we became young teenagers, they all advised us never, never to park with a boy at Piedmont Park, the large park near Grady High School. This was dangerous! They said if we wanted to park and kiss, we should park in one of their driveways so we would be safe.

EDITH AND ALVIN TOWNLEY, SR., 1990. MRS. TOWNLEY
WAS ONE OF THE "MORNINGSIDE MOTHERS."

But seriously, these wonderful mothers modeled for all of us what mothers should be like, and I will be forever grateful for them and to them. As I remember them today, it gives new meaning to "it takes a village." Thanks to my friends' mothers, I slowly learned what "normal" was in a family. I never felt excluded or deprived because they saw to it. None of the mothers ever asked me about my home life, although I'm sure they knew. They were sure that I had a costume if we were in a play. They made sure that I was included when we took ballroom dancing at the Georgian Terrace Hotel in downtown Atlanta. Mrs. Townley fed me more than one Sunday night supper on their front porch with Janice. Janice was so skinny then—just sticks! I remember that she would make Janice a milkshake with an egg beat up in it to try to fatten her up a little. She would serve that to Janice with our dinner.

I always felt God's love, protection and presence in my young life, and I knew that I had a choice in the things I chose to do. At the time it seemed to me that my "not-so-perfect childhood" would carry into my adulthood and I wouldn't have any choices, but I knew I did. I knew it was completely up to me. I thought about what advice I would have given my "young self" when I was a teenager. Mine was, "Everything will be alright one day." Occasionally I'll ask a friend what advice she would give her "young self" and sometimes the friend will say, "I wouldn't have gotten married so young." Or, "I wouldn't have married my first husband." No one regrets having gone to college or following their dreams. So, dream on! God has *wonderful* plans in store.

CHAPTER 19

The Fabulous 50s

Whoo Hoo! High School! The best time of my life, growing up. Henry Grady High School was a great place to be in the fifties and a great place to be a teenager. Whatever was lacking at home, high school filled in for me. Our Grady mascot was the Gray Knight. We were the Grady Gray Knights! My father, a professional musician, was positive that surely I could learn to play *something* in the band. *Anything*. As a matter of fact, I tried the clarinet, accordion, violin and the piano. I can still play a little piano, and since I know the notes, I have been able to sing in Methodist church choirs for twenty-five years, but the true musical ability was not inherited by me. What I really wanted to be was a majorette in high school, so I could wear the skimpy little white satin outfit and show off my legs. Daddy refused to let me be a majorette unless I learned to play *something*. So, finally, we found the glocken-spiel, which is a xylophone which hangs around your neck with these long, orange horsehair tails hanging from each side. This was extremely embarrassing, but hey, it enabled me to play during concert season and be a majorette during football season. It satisfied my father, anyway. The band trips were so much fun. There was one other girl in the band who played glockenspiel named Linda Christmas. She was better than I was, but the two of us had a solo in *America the Beautiful*. Only the two of us played "And the Rockets' Red Glare, the Bombs Bursting in Air..."

GRADY HIGH SCHOOL,

929 CHARLES ALLEN DRIVE, ATLANTA, NEXT TO PIEDMONT PARK

Grady had a wonderful mixed chorus too, and along with some dancers at school, put on some good plays. Gilbert and Sullivan operettas were popular. Mr. Seitz, director of the band and orchestra, and "Doc" Rumble, director of the mixed chorus, were popular with the students, and the performances were an enjoyable part of Grady High School.

Our school was a wonderful mix of Jewish kids, Greek kids, and Protestant kids. We all got along well and were like brothers and sisters. There were no gangs, no fighting, and no bullying. I am not making this up. I do not remember even one incident of bullying.

Our class keeps up with each other with our reunions, which have gotten closer together now as we are getting older faster, it seems, and we have lost some of our schoolmates. Now we sometimes meet for lunch at Mary Mac's, which was one of our favorites in high school. It is well attended by our class. Our chief planners are our classmates Phyllis Miller Hahn, Bonnie Isenberg Richmond, and Helaine Kaufman Buchwald. They have tirelessly kept up with everyone and planned our reunions. Thank you, girls. I have so many close friends from Grady. Also, many of our teachers came back to our reunions too, until we lost them all.

My husband, Noah, who went to school in Baltimore, doesn't remember one single person from high school. A pity! *And* he doesn't remember any camp songs either. Not even *Kukuboro Sat in the Old Gum Tree.*

One day while I was in the 10th grade, Daddy came home and announced that we were going to move to Sandy Springs,

Georgia, which I considered at the time to be the "country." At that time, there was no I-285, the perimeter interstate that circles the city, and Sandy Springs was mostly a graveled road to Roswell, Georgia. This was also a big surprise to my stepmother, Dixie, whom he married when I turned twelve. The house itself was lovely on a lake on Lake Forest Drive, but everything about it, including everything about Sandy Springs, was alien to me. I put my foot down and refused to move…but of course I had to. Where else can you go when you are fifteen? Grady High School allowed me to drive back and forth from Sandy Springs, and I had a couple of fellow students who rode with me. Their parents had moved to the North of Atlanta also. So, all worked out okay.

Sandy Springs was sparsely populated with one small group of stores. There was a dime store where my Uncle Stan Lacy was the manager. The main grocery store was a little stucco building which had a one-armed butcher named Mr. Burdette. He was a long time resident of Sandy Springs, and he was a member of a pioneer family. There is a road named after him in Sandy Springs. There were so few cars in the sparsely populated neighborhood that I wouldn't even call it traffic. My brother, Larry, had a Moped motorized bicycle, and he rode me all over Sandy Springs on it.

My girlfriends and I had plenty of boy friends—not boyfriends. Our girlfriends' circle of friends at Grady included guys that we felt comfortable with, and our parents felt comfortable with them too. We had some fun dances and proms at Grady, and everybody usually had a date. Once we had a "twerp dance" where the girls invited the boys and made them a corsage out of vegetables. The girls' fathers picked up the boys for the date. Our formal gowns for the proms were constructed of tons and tons of net. We did not wear sophisticated slinky gowns; in fact, we were definitely not sophisticated by today's standards. Our dances were the jitterbug and the shag, and of course s-l-o-w dancing. The boys brought us corsages of carnations, or if the couple really liked each other, he might give her a small orchid.

We definitely got to see and listen to all the cool bands: The Platters, The Drifters, Fats Domino, and Elvis. *The Ed Sullivan Show* that I remember most is when Elvis made his first TV appearance. The show was in black and white. Janice and I watched it in her basement with her dog Cute Babes. They had to black out his pelvis on the screen with a black box because he was the first one to do a bump and grind on TV. Later, Janice and I saved up our collection money, which was meant for church, and we went on the bus downtown to see Elvis in person when he came to Atlanta. He was probably about nineteen years old, just at the beginning of his career. He sang *(You Ain't Nothin' But A) Hound Dog*, and we thought we would die. We reacted and screamed just like the clips from TV. Shows like *The Jackie Gleason Show* which seemed very funny at the time aren't funny at all now. We all used to like *The Twilight Zone*, which was the first of its kind.

DEBS SOCIAL CLUB, GRADY HIGH SCHOOL, 1956

My father insisted on meeting all of my dates. They were to park, come in the house, and talk to him before we left on our date. The problem was by the time the boy came to pick me up, Daddy was passed out in his chair, unable to meet anybody. I was so embarrassed, I managed to pull him out of the chair, take him by the feet and drag him around the corner of the living room so that my date would not see him.

In high school, the girls had to wear skirts or dresses with sweaters with detachable Peter Pan collars. No pants! For Saturday, we wore blue jeans, which we called "dungarees." There were no designer labels except for Levis. We wore saddle oxfords back in the early 50s and penny loafers later, and still later, ballerina slippers with bulky white bobby socks. During the ballerina slipper phase, we wore big skirts with petticoats under them. Some girls starched their petticoats, but we happened on the idea of flexible plastic screening from the hardware store, and we made our slips out of this stuff! For school, every girl had at least one cashmere sweater, sometimes given to you for Christmas by a serious boyfriend. Another popular gift was a necklace with a floating opal pendant or a mustard seed pendant. Make-up was pretty minimal. There was a lipstick called Tangee that was supposed to change color on you—the very color you wanted. Hairspray was very popular. There was no tattooing or body piercing except for piercing your ears, and this was usually just the bad girls at that time. The worst thing you could do was streak your hair peroxide blond or pierce your ears. Those girls were cheap!

GRADY GRADUATING CLASS, 1957

As I mentioned before, about the time I entered Grady High School, Daddy married a woman named Dixie. As far as any of us knew, she had never been married and had no children. She had no wish to have any either. He met her when he called on the State of Georgia as a customer for the printing company. She worked in a lab that dealt with seeds in Georgia. She did not like Larry or me, and she had no mothering skills that I ever saw. As we say in the South, "She would rather lie than tell the truth." Of course, life with Daddy must have come as a shock, and I'm sure she didn't expect an alcoholic. At first she did not drink with Daddy, just got into fights with him, but as time went on, she joined him in his drinking. He did not physically abuse her, however, as he did my mother, and at the time he died at age 63, they had been married for ten years.

I think the happiest day of her life was when I left for college. The next time I came home from college for a weekend, she had switched my brand new bathrobe for her worn out one—they were identical, given to us by Daddy for Christmas. There were many just mean things like her saying, "I bought you the cutest white leather jacket today, but somebody stole it out of the back seat of the car." Larry was at home during the summers at this time. One night he left a note for me on my pillow to come down to his bedroom after my date. His bedroom was on the lower level. She had gotten mad at him and scratched his face with her long fingernails. Both of his cheeks had long red streaks down them. I barged into Daddy's bedroom and told Daddy that it was either her or me. He could pick. He put her suitcase out in the carport. After a few days she came back, but at least I took up for poor Larry.

She lived for about ten more years. At the time of her death, we received the news from her attorney that she had had an out-of-wedlock son and had changed her name before coming to Atlanta. This son had pre-deceased her, but he had left four children in Atlanta who questioned the will. It was like a soap opera or *The Twilight Zone*, and it was a very difficult time for me. I was sure that being a good businessman, Daddy had written his will with legal help and exactly as he wanted it. Larry was living in Florida and wasn't able to help me deal with this except for keeping in touch with our attorney. I'm sure that Daddy never knew about her child, and he had tried to be so careful about planning his estate, much of which was lost to attorneys and to Dixie's surprise family. I am not the only one to have experienced a bizarre turn of events like this, but it was a shock! The Executor of the Will was the C&S Bank, but thank goodness Uncle Honey had been named as consultant, and he carried a big stick. He managed to get the C&S Bank to go ahead and release what was left to Larry and me after our battle with Dixie's grandchildren.

During my whole senior year at Grady, Jim and I dated, and I really wanted to get married instead of going to college. However, my father had another idea and promised us that if I would just go to college for one year, if I still wanted to get married, he would agree. So, off I went to the University of Georgia in 1957.

I roomed with my Cousin Bobbie, and we took all of the same classes. We joined the Alpha Gamma Delta Sorority, and we went to services at our favorite church in Athens on Sundays, which was, at the time, an Episcopal church. At the end of that year, Jim and I approached Daddy again to live up to his bargain, and he agreed, although I was just nineteen. Thinking back on the whole time, I wanted to get away from home very badly. If things had been different, I might have continued at Georgia.

Cousins Bobbie and Lynne, Alpha Gamma Delta sorority photos

Bobbie and I had a wonderful time rooming together. Her Mother, Bee, would send us delicious cakes and cookies from home, which were placed in our mail cubbies on the first floor of our dorm. We would come back from class to see several girls waiting around our cubby to see what she had sent, hoping to have a bite. We would store these goodies in our closet in our room sometimes, but we never left the door locked and friends on our floor would come in and raid our closet!

We had a very strict dorm mother. Some of the boys on campus staged a "panty raid" one night. Bobbie and I were so excited. We were on the third floor and probably would have fainted if a boy had made it up to that level. We did hold up panties in the window and shook them up and down. Our dorm mother called the Fire Department, which came to our dorm and hosed the poor boys off the lawn.

It was also during this 1957-1958 year that I met Mary Ann Lawler from California, who became engaged to Gary Beaufait. She became one of my lifelong friends, one of our trio of Barbara Theus, Mary Ann Beaufait, and Lynne Byrd.

After I left to get married, my cousin Bobbie stayed on for another year, living in the Alpha Gamma Delta House. She married John Sherrod, who had his degree in Forestry from the University of Georgia. After they married, John's job as a Forest Ranger took him to many areas far and wide, such as the Dakotas, Alaska, and Oregon. He took my cousin away from me!

CHAPTER 20

Real and Imagined Careers

My first job as a teen was working in the drug store in Sandy Springs making sodas and frying hamburgers. It was a specific job to earn money for a prom dress. We had the old-fashioned milk shake blenders, and one night the janitor mopped the floor and it was wet. I started to make a milk shake and got a terrific electric shock. No harm done; prom dress was bought and worn to prom!

My next job was working with my cousin Bobbie during the summers at our fathers' printing company on Parkway Drive, The Harry Barfield Printing Company. We would do office work and errands, pretending we were our daddies' secretaries. Back in those days, girls wouldn't have thought of taking over their father's companies, and their fathers wouldn't have thought of it either. Now, they would. My cousin Billie did work for them as a graphic artist after she later finished college at the University of Georgia. She is very artistic and was a great graphic artist.

During this time I was in love with TV shows about medicine; *Dr. Ben Casey* was one of them. I was fascinated with medicine, and I wanted to work at Georgia Baptist the summer that I was a junior at Grady. I would walk from Grady to Georgia Baptist after school, which was about 2 miles, and I would beg them to hire me. They explained that I was only 15 and didn't have a Social Security card, so it was impossible. I did wear them down however, and they hired me for the summer. I was 15 for a few weeks and when I turned 16 in June, they hired me and paid me minimum wage. I fancied myself as a doctor one day, and so did my cousin, Bobbie. My first pay check was $60—a fortune! The hospital paid all of the employees once a month, and many of the workers had families. That last week before payday was hard for them. My duties in the Admissions Office were to type a metal plate on a machine called the Addressograph. This plate was used to stamp all of the paperwork for the patients with name and hospital number. I was still working at Georgia Baptist when I was first married, and by that time I had transferred to Medical Records where I began to learn medical terminology.

I really liked medical transcription, and soon they put me on it fulltime. It was great practice to have interns and doctors from other cultures with different accents, even back at that time! It turned out to be a great springboard for me, and after that, I worked for several different doctors and groups.

The first one was in 1961 at the Atlanta Psychiatric Clinic: Doctors Thomas Malone, Richard Felder, John Warkentin, Rives Chalmers, Herb Stone, Ellen Kiser, Bill Kiser, Tom Leland, and Carl Whitaker. Psychiatry was in its infancy in Atlanta in the early 60's. It was my great privilege to meet Dr. Hervey Cleckley, who co-authored *The Three Faces of Eve,* the true story of a patient with three distinct personalities; Dr. Carl Rogers, the Father of child- or person-centered therapy, the Rogerian Theory, and many others. Dr. Carl Whitaker and Dr. Thomas Malone co-authored the classic *The Roots of Psychotherapy.* Our patients were some of Atlanta's most prominent citizens. This was the beginning of the John Kennedy Era, and I remember all the staff and doctors watching the inauguration of John Kennedy on TV in our main office. I had commented, "Gee, Mr. Kennedy doesn't look nervous at all!" and Dr. Malone had called my attention to his hands, which were slightly shaking and twitching, hanging at his side.

The next medical job I had was as a secretary and assistant to Dr. John Akin, a general surgeon in Atlanta who practiced at Piedmont Hospital. He had just brought Dr. Carl R. Hartrampf, Jr. into the practice, when I started to work. In 1962, I was 23 years old and Dr. Hartrampf was 31, just beginning his practice in general surgery.

Dr. Hartrampf's true dream was to take and pass his Plastic Surgery Boards and become one of Atlanta's first plastic surgeons; Atlanta only had four plastic surgeons in 1962. After about a year, Dr. Hartrampf and I had to move to another office in the Sheffield Building so that he could concentrate on plastic surgery and his Plastic Surgery Boards, and it was my honor to type them for him. His office nurse, Barbara Ballenger, and I had them bound for him. He later opened The Atlanta Plastic Surgery Clinic in Atlanta. This was a wonderful time in my work life, and Dr. Hartrampf and his surgical nurse, Sarah Simmons, were two of the sweetest, kindest, and most dedicated people I have ever known. Dr. Hartrampf later pioneered the remarkable breast surgery for female cancer patients called the Pedicle TRAM Flap, making it possible for a woman to have breasts made of her own abdominal body tissue. He designed it on paper and first performed it on a cadaver, and then on a volunteer breast cancer patient. He himself was recovering from surgery when he planned this operation. After that operation, which was filmed, he taught one doctor at a time, and they, in turn, taught others. This particular surgery is very popular now for breast cancer patients. It was a huge success and a blessing to so many women.

Having two small boys during this time, I would occasionally drop out of working for a few months and then go back. At one point I worked at home, collecting tapes of transcription, typing them at home, and delivering them back to the service or to the doctor. One time I had worked all morning when Dixon was in kindergarten and Dave was napping, and I had my transcription neatly organized on the bed of the bedroom I where I was working. At about 12:15 that day, Dixon flew into the house and said, "I'm home, Mom!" and he dove on top of the bed where my morning's work was located! "Eeeeeee,"

I said. I ended up ironing the work, and it was good as new when I delivered it.

Over the years I would work for Dr. Akin and Dr. Hartrampf, as well as their friends at The Children's' Clinical Center: Doctors Judson Hawk (Dr. Akin's cousin), Dr. Joe Snitzer, Dr. Walter Murray, Dr. Keller Carlock, and Dr. Jimmy Brown. When I was hired at The Children's Clinical Center, I explained to Dr. Hawk that if my children were sick, I would not be able to come to work. Dr. Hawk said, "That's no problem at all. We'll just save one of the examining rooms for whoever is sick, and he will have a TV in there and you can check on him all day." So, done! This office was busy, busy, busy, and we had a lot of kids coming in. Dixon grew taller than Dr. Hawk and asked him, "What happens when I'm too long for this table?" And Dr. Hawk said, "Oh, we just trim a little off your feet..." But seriously, mothers would bring them in until they had adult blood pressures. All of these doctors were wonderful and dedicated, and I loved them all. I was thrilled when Dr. Jimmy Brown joined us because he and I had gone to Grady together and played in the Grady Band. He was one class behind me. Dr. Brown played a mean clarinet!

I also worked at The Shallowford Hospital in Medical Records and as Assistant to the CEO of Scottish Rite Children's' Hospital (now Children's' Healthcare of Atlanta) and the CEO of St. Joseph's Hospital (now Emory at St. Joseph's).

This covered the space of twenty-five years and was my first career. I thoroughly enjoyed all of these jobs, and sometimes I felt like I was passed around between them when they needed me. I never had to look for a job. I'd just call them, and they would make a place for me.

Maybe everybody at one time or another thinks they can be a writer. I had had pretty good success in my Creative Writing Class after going back to college at Georgia State University in 1994, and since I had been in the medical field for a long time, I had an idea that I would write a story for *The Atlanta Journal* as a freelance writer about a new medical school at Mercer University in Macon. It was the first year for this program, which was open to students who wished to get a medical degree, but were perhaps older, married with children, wanted another career, or were otherwise not the usual first year medical student.

"How interesting," I thought. So, without confirming the newspaper's interest, I called the school and explained that I was a freelance writer and wanted to do a story on their new medical school. They were delighted! So I dressed up in my best suit and arrived at Macon to find that they had rolled out the red carpet for me. I met the President of the School, as well as other doctors and teachers, and they had set up rooms with students at work or in labs with their microscopes, or learning other things. I realized that they thought I was associated with the AJC, and I got a tremendous stress headache. It was quite a day. A very, very long day. They even supplied a photographer who made pictures of the whole day as I furiously wrote notes. I was covered in perspiration by the end of the day, ready to drop, and wondering if they might arrest me for being an imposter. The AJC was not interested in the article, but I was so traumatized that this appeared to me to be the beginning and the end of my writing career, although I am now giving it another try in an entirely different way! I am sorry to say that I threw away the pictures the school sent me to go with my story, but I'm sure they have copies because they would be a part of the school's history.

I have always enjoyed my medical jobs, but I suffered a lot of guilt because I left the boys with babysitters. When they were born, most of the mothers stayed home and didn't work. Good childcare was hard to come by, and I left them in some childcare centers that I wouldn't consider today. Jim and I thought that we needed for me to work, so I did. Maybe if we had thought it over more we could have figured out how I could have stayed home. We did manage to include Boy Scouts, Cub Scouts, soccer, bicycling, vacations, and guitar for the boys, and just about anything mechanical as far as hobbies for both of them. At any rate, they are both great guys and are doing well, now both in their fifties. Both are very technologically-oriented. My last job, from which I retired in April of 2015, was a "God Job." Dr. Pete Hutchings, a Psychologist, and I had been Stephen Ministers together for nine years at Dunwoody United Methodist Church. We, our fellow Stephen Ministers, and our Pastor, Dr. Wiley Stephens, thought that we needed a Counseling Center to serve anyone who needed counseling. We prayed for this Center for four years, and in 2010, our prayers were answered, and we opened the Dunwoody United Methodist Counseling Center in the Amacher Office Complex next door to the church.

While we were beginning our fourth year, our Advisory Board was forced to re-evaluate our sustainability, as we were helping many who could not otherwise afford counseling. We operated on a sliding-scale based on yearly salary. However, many clients were without a job and were seen at low cost or no cost. We had a total of three counselors: Dr. Pete Hutchings, psychologist and Director; Dr. Scott Hutchings, an ordained Minister and specialist in drug counseling; and Rev. Stephanie Holmes, an ordained Minister and specialist in Autism and Asperger's Syndrome. I decided at this point to retire since I had turned 75 and had so many things I wanted to do in retirement. And after all, "there weren't too many shopping days until Christmas!" No one can really predict how long their life will be.

CHAPTER 21

Marrying My Childhood Sweetheart

On my off day while working at my first real job at Georgia Baptist Hospital in the Admissions Office, the hospital called and asked, "Lynne, can you come in today? The regular Sunday admissions girl is sick." I had been swimming in our lake, and my hair was soaking wet, but I went in to work. The Head of Admissions brought me an admissions form and winked and said, "This boy is really cute." So after I had made his plate on the Addressograph, I called his name to go to the laboratory for his blood work: "Jim Patrick."

He *was* cute! He was tall and lanky with a crew cut, blue eyes, and a nice smile. I was attracted to him immediately, but couldn't figure out how I could go and see him. Remember, girls *must* be introduced first. He was being admitted for a surgical procedure called a hemorrhoidectomy. How embarrassing for him, and how we laughed about it later when we dated with his cushion!

JIM PATRICK, DATING DAYS, 1959

Later that day, his father came down to Admissions and introduced himself and asked if I would visit his son after surgery. It turned out that our fathers were both Shriners, and in fact played in the Shrine band together. Not only that, but my friend Nancy's father was the pastor of Jim's church. It seemed like it was meant to be.

I had been raised as Methodist, but Jim was Christian (Disciples of Christ denomination). We both felt that it was important that we be united in one denomination. So I was baptized in the Christian Church—Methodists sprinkle and other denominations dunk—so I had to be dunked because they wouldn't accept my sprinkling. Dr. Harrison McMains, Nancy's father, married us in the Historic First Christian Church downtown in 1958. We were the last couple to be married in that old church at the corner of Trinity and Pryor Street. Shortly after, the church was demolished, and an ugly parking lot took its place. Every time I think about that, I experience a blow in my preservationist's stomach! At that time, our Mayor of Atlanta, Maynard Jackson, thought of historic buildings as "Hunks of Junk." I don't believe today that they would tear down such a beautiful old church.

When we were married, I was barely nineteen and Jim was twenty-one. Daddy drove me to the church on my wedding day, and all the way he kept saying, "You can change your mind! It's not too late!" I was sitting in the back seat, the whole back seat taken up with my beautiful white fluffy wedding gown. I was so in love. No one could have talked me out of getting married that day. My cousin, Bobbie, was my Maid of Honor and my friends Nancy McMains, Janice Townley, Virginia Smith, and Annetta McConnell were my brides-maids. I bought my wedding dress from Rich's for $100, and my veil for $15. Because we purchased the wedding dress and all of the bridesmaids dresses at Rich's, the Rich's consultant actually came out to conduct the wedding. Dr. McMains, Nancy's father and our pastor, wanted to know why we didn't ask him to sing at the wedding too. He said, "I could have just stepped two steps to the side and sang your song for you!" Back in that day, receptions were much simpler than today. We had a wedding cake, punch, salted nuts, and little decorated teacakes. Today, wedding receptions include huge buffets of food with elaborate decorations and drink stations, and sometimes a band.

Every new bride registered at Rich's and Davison's, both of which later became Macy's. There were no other registrations in places like Home Depot or Crate and Barrel, or Target. Brides usually received one "good" plate in their pattern, or one silver fork or spoon, or a silver-plated serving dish of some kind. Everybody my age has a bunch of silver or silver-plated things that they never use and don't know what to do with. We all hate polishing silver at this point in our lives. Give me stainless steel and pottery dishes!

We went on our honeymoon to Chattanooga, Tennessee, at the top of Lookout Mountain, and we went through the caverns there. We also enjoyed the gorgeous view from the top of the mountain. We purchased our first "See Rock City" birdhouse while we were there and also bought a couple of fairy crosses, which are Christian crosses which are naturally formed and mined in the area. We also went to Ruby Falls, another attraction in the area with an underground cavern with a large waterfall.

CHAPTER 22

Babies Having Babies, Part #1

When I found out I was pregnant, Jim was working part-time at Lay's Potato Chip Company on Peachtree Industrial Boulevard. I took two different buses each work day to get to Georgia Baptist Hospital. By that time, I had progressed to medical transcription at the hospital and had become proficient in the different specialties. I was still nineteen and in the dark about having a baby.

To illustrate just how in the dark I was, I picked out my obstetrician by riding down Peachtree Street on a Saturday morning until I saw a doctor's office. I parked, went in to the receptionist, and explained that I thought I might be pregnant. I had only missed a couple of days of my anticipated period. I ended up staying with this same doctor, Dan Kahle, for the birth of Dixon, and later, Dave. Jim and I were poorish at the time as he was still going to school, so when I was about six months pregnant, we moved in with his parents. I gained 50 lbs. with Dixon, and I was really, really big. Granny and Pop Patrick, his parents, were wonderful to us, but I didn't like living with them. We had only been married for a year, and I felt like Jim was back home with his parents, and I was "the girlfriend." We were both young and immature.

In 1959, there was no ultrasound, and a new young mother didn't know the sex of her baby until it was born. Dixon was born two weeks earlier than anticipated. When I realized I was in labor, I got up, dressed, and put my coat on. Jim woke up and said, "Where are you going?" I said, "I think I'm in labor," to which he said, "But you have two more weeks." We had no idea that babies came when they are ready—early or late. Talk about dumb.

Back then, the fathers were treated like lepers. They couldn't come into the labor or delivery room, and they couldn't get anywhere near the baby. In the labor room, there was another mother next to me in the later stages of labor who scared me to death. She was screaming in Spanish for her mother. My doctor came in, patted my hand, and told me that he and Jim were going across the street for breakfast, and they would be back later since I was in early labor. I could not believe they would desert me when I was in labor!

When Dixon was born on October 22, 1959 after a long labor, he had a cone head. We didn't know to expect this, and we thought something was wrong. We thought he would go through life with a cone head. We wanted to give him four

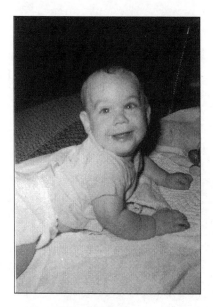

JAMES DIXON PATRICK, JR.
(DICKIE), 3 MONTHS OLD, 1959

names, but my father had a conniption fit, which is when someone in the South goes temporarily insane and can't be reasoned with. He said that four names would give him trouble all of his life. He said when he went in the military, they couldn't handle four names. I couldn't conceive of this little baby ever going in the military, which he later did before going to college—the Air Force. He ended up with the name Dixon, which is his fraternal grandmother's maiden name. My father cried when Dixon was born, which was the only time I ever saw him cry about anything. It touched me deeply.

I had a roommate at Georgia Baptist Hospital who had delivered her second baby. They brought our babies to us at the same time in our shared hospital room. She took her baby's diaper off and turned him all around and inspected him, but I was afraid to even touch mine. He stayed right where the nurse left him when she brought him. My doctor talked me into trying to nurse, and I agreed. The next thing I knew, my room had filled with brand new student nurses to watch me try to nurse. It didn't work at all. How embarrassing!

JIM AND DICKIE, 4, AT THE CARTERSVILLE FARM, 1963

CHAPTER 23

Babies Having Babies, Part #2

We moved from Granny and Pop Patrick's back to the Oglethorpe apartments for a while when Dixon was about three months old. Granny Patrick had become used to caring for the baby, and when I went to pick him up one day, she was reluctant to give him to me. So we moved to a duplex in Chamblee on Pearl Lane.

We were so thrilled to have our privacy, and a carport for our one car, a luxury for us. The duplex was attached to its twin, and the family who lived there had a little boy who was a great playmate for Dixon. It was also closer to the bus stop. Jim had to use our car to get to work, and the bus was now easier for me to take to work. We thought we had died and gone to heaven. The duplex was completely made of concrete blocks. In the kitchen, we decorated them with plastic brick-looking wallpaper, which would peel off the wall during the night from the humidity. We would have to stick it back up every morning.

One Christmas on Pearl Lane when Dixon was about eighteen months old, the encyclopedia salesman came to the door and convinced us that Dixon needed a set of encyclopedias and that a yearly update book would take care of all the changes. This was years before he even started school! Anyway, we bought them and a bookcase to put them in. It seems funny now that anyone can go on the Internet and find anything without ever looking at an encyclopedia. It's even possible to hear someone reading the information and see a moving picture of it.

While we were on Pearl Lane, we found out that Dave was on the way. I worked until I was about seven months pregnant, then I stayed home with Dixon, waiting for the new baby. Every afternoon Dickie and I would walk up to Buford Highway and get a treat at the shopping center, usually a doughnut. It is a good memory.

Jim and I then decided it was time for a house, and we built the house on 2464 Ridgeway Drive in Doraville. Jim's parents had given us $10,000 and mine gave us $5,000, and we were able to build a house for a total of $19,000. This was a lot of money in 1962. Our interest rate was 4%. The house sat back off the road and had a beautiful wooded front yard. It was built on two acres. We built the house sitting in the middle of a dirt area, planning later to do fancy landscaping. The house itself was small with three small bedrooms. I could plug in the vacuum cleaner in the hallway and vacuum the whole house without moving the cord to another location.

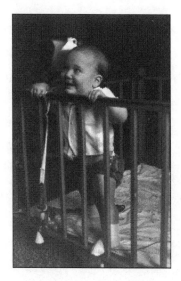

DAVID PATRICK, 1963

Brother Dave was born June 30, 1962. He was a robust, happy baby who also spent a lot of time sleeping. I took him to the pediatrician, complaining that Dave slept all the time, and he was just too good to be true. Dr. Hawk looked at me and said, "Typical second baby. He's fine!"

When I brought Dave home and put him in the baby bed so I could sit and visit with his grandparents in the living room, we noticed that big brother Dickie was missing. We heard a pitiful newborn cry and went running into the bedroom to find that Dickie had piled all of his toys on top of his little brother. He looked at me and said, "I share!"

It took a while for me to learn to be a mother. I had zero experience with babies, and it did not seem to come naturally. We called Dixon "Dickie" and "Dick" until he came home one day from school in the first grade and said, "Mom, don't call me 'Big Dick' anymore. I can't tell you why."

We also thought David looked like a little possum when he was born, and we called him "Possum." When it was time for kindergarten, his teacher called me at home and said, "Mrs. Patrick, can you *please* call your son by his Christian name? He thinks his name is Possum. If the police should ask him, he would say, 'My name is Possum Patrick and I live on Ridgeway Drive.'"

My brother Larry lived with us for a short time when he was in college and was there when Dave was born. A friend of his babysat with Dixon. Larry was always a big help, enjoyed the boys, and we missed him when he decided to live on campus.

We had a lot of fun and happy memories with the boys, one of which was when we raised Dalmatian puppies. Our Mama Dalmatian was named Lady. She had a litter of fourteen puppies! The Dalmatian breed has a reputation for deafness and some cleft palates in some dogs. One little adorable puppy had a cleft palate, and I immediately named her Shrinking Violet. I stayed up with her trying to get her to take some milk from a dropper, but she didn't make it and we lost her the first night, making the litter thirteen.

Dalmatians grow quickly, and they had to have their shots and check-ups, so I took them to the vet in pillow cases, three to a pillow case—okay, one pillowcase had four. The vet would pull one out of the pillow case and shoot it in the butt and then put it on the floor and pull out another one. Soon there were little peeing black spotted puppies all over the room.

We enjoyed selling them inexpensively to people we liked. They were all registered, and the breeder had told us not to give one away, even if we just charged $25. She said people just appreciate things more when they have an investment in them. One couple in particular had almost no money, and the pup they liked the most was so eager to greet you that he had run into a snag in the fence and had a small scar on his head near his ear. They explained that "We really can't afford a purebred puppy, but we so want this one!" So we let them have him for $10.00. They reported to us regularly and said that he slept in the bed between them and now he was so big that he would stretch his four legs out and they had a hard time getting together!

DIXON AND DAVID WITH LADY, 1966

As I explained, our house had been built right in the middle of red dirt. The driveway was gravel for a long stretch, and the house sat at the back of the property. The landscaping we had saved for a day when we could afford it. One day Jim and I were on his father's tractor, trying to clear out some trees in the back yard, and we set the woods on fire. I can't remember how, but we had to call the fire department to put out the fire. Those trees lived, but had scorched bases for years.

DIXON AND DAVID PATRICK, 1968, RIDGEWAY DRIVE, DORAVILLE

The boys were great friends and did a lot of things together. Both were very mechanical and loved riding bikes together, repairing things, putting batteries and propellers on anything, even an old piece of wood. They entertained one another at the table, nicknaming each other "Mumbles and Grumbles" and having "bed sales." Bed sales were when they put everything they wanted to get rid of on their beds and then sold their stuff to each other. They never got in trouble in school and both had a lot of friends. As they got older, they enjoyed motorcycles and we had a track in the front yard with whoop-de-doos, which were things to jump over. They did a lot of trail biking. As an older teenager, David started playing the guitar and enjoyed it for many years. Dixon tells me that my memory is bad, that they weren't perfect kids, but they almost were.

Both boys graduated from North Springs High School. I must explain that about the time Dixon entered first grade, we began to suspect that he might have some sort of learning problem. He was always in motion. I remember peeking through the window on the door of the first grade room. His leg and foot were going up and down, ninety miles an hour, and he was busy talking to his neighbor. He had a lot of trouble learning to read and spell. At the time he was having so many problems, but we knew nothing about learning disabilities. A group of parents banded together and shared stories about the problems our children were having. We went to some seminars, did some research, and opened our own little learning disability school, which we held after regular school during the week. We learned that some children learn by hearing, some were visual, and some could learn to spell by lightly using a finger touching sand paper. Dixon was one who learned by hearing.

We would talk to groups of parents and illustrate that if a fish, a bird, and a dog were in the same class, then the fish would make an A in swimming, but not do so well in flying or barking. The dog would make an A in barking, but not do so well in flying. In other words, children learn differently. This little group, I'm proud to say, was instrumental in the legislation that now requires all prospective teachers to have a course in learning disabilities.

So when Dixon was in high school, I recorded his lessons in reading, and he would listen to them. When he went to college after high school, the administration was not interested in any special teaching for any one student. They explained that they "taught to the norm." So after going to college for a short time, Dixon went into the Air Force where he learned electrical skills. When he got out, he went to DeVry University, graduated at the top of his class and was recruited by Sandia Laboratories in Albuquerque, New Mexico. After a career fair at the school, they flew him and four others for interviews, then the night of his graduation, they called and offered him the job. He has worked for the company for twenty-six years. He has gone to Europe and other countries to work on security designs for government contracts. He is the only employee in his field who was promoted to Professional Engineer without having a four-year college degree.

Dixon met and married native Atlantan Zelda, a lovely daughter of the prominent Dunwoody Amacher Family after he was discharged from the Air Force. They have two daughters. Samantha, 30, and Brenda, 28, who both live in Albuquerque.

People with learning disabilities are often very intelligent with high I.Q.'s. Following is a story that Dixon wrote in the fourth grade called "I am a Cent." It is very hard to decipher by looking at the original, because the spelling is all wrong. But you can tell by the content what an imagination he has and how intelligent he is.

DIXON GRADUATES FROM DEVRY UNIVERSITY,

PICTURED WITH NOAH, 1988

I Am a Cent
by Dixon Patrick

When I first became a coin, I was made in San Francisco, 1944. I wasn't the only one; there were millions and millions of us. I was in bag number 222 with about 2 or 3 thousand more around me. I was on the side of the bag near the top. "Hold It!" I hear someone coming. "Hey, Tom!" "Yes, Fred sent bags 13 through 250 to the shipping dock." "O.K.," said Tom. "Hey Fred, where are the coins going?" "They're going to the San Francisco banks downtown." After having this discussion I wanted to go and see the world! So on Dec 6, 1944, I was taken out of the bag. The teller said, "Thank you," and in the man's change, guess who? Later, you know I'm at the bottom of this guy's pocket and it's dark under all these papers. I want to see the world! When the man got home his son said, "Tomorrow is Saturday and it is allowance time!" The father said, "O.K. son, here you go — one day early!" "Thanks Dad." I'm going to get a piece of gum at the gum machine on the corner. After hearing that, I was not going to let it happen — so I was going to organize a little accident to happen! He was about to put me in, when he did it anyway! How could he do this to me? I want to see the world — maybe an aerial view but guess I can talk to my friends down here. But at that same time, the boy dropped the gum on the sidewalk and it rolled onto the street. A car chased the boy and hit the gum machine. All the coins went in the air and I was rolling down Main Street. Help! I'm falling down the sewer all down, down, down. I was (floating?) so the top of the water in the sewer had ice on top of it. I am floating all through the sewer all night that stunk. In the morning there was a light _____. Before I know it, I am on a stream. There was a fire ahead. Two sewer men were talking about something. One man, Sam, said "It's sure cold." The other, Tony, said, "It sure is. There is something on that piece of ice. It's a coin!" Sam said, "Bug Off!" Tony went to see about it. The next day, Tony, Sam and me, Yours Truly. Oh, this is a hold up and Sam is on the way ___ car with some money. Tony came when Sam was running out of the bank, and I fell out of his pocket and landed in cement and after that I've been stuck in the cement. "The robbers got away but, but the world can come to me."

* * *

Neither Dixon nor I could figure out what the scribbled words were where we've left the blanks.

Dixon got a "B" on the paper with expressions of "Great! Very Creative, Very Imaginative!" along with advice to always keep a dictionary by his side. But how can you look up something if you have spelled "accident" as "assadent"?

Dave graduated from Georgia Southern University with an Industrial Technology degree and has worked in the IT field in Atlanta, Nashville, and now in Colorado Springs, Colorado.

DAVE GRADUATING FROM GEORGIA SOUTHERN UNIVERSITY, 1985

137

Dave inherited my father's music talent and began playing the guitar at an early age. He played guitar at Georgia Southern and sang with a Wesley musical group called "A New Mind." He also played guitar in the Gazebo at the Opryland Hotel in Nashville and recorded several CDs with his original music. His other hobbies include running, motorcycle riding, and bicycling. Dave has always been very physically fit, loving to run in marathons and half-marathons. One summer, he bicycled across Iowa with friends. He has designed several enhancements for musical instruments and has applied for a patent for an inexpensive, fold-up amp holder. He decided to move, and before leaving Nashville, he purchased a fifth-wheel camper with all the bells and whistles and set out to visit different states. He said, "When I came to Colorado, I knew I was home." He enjoys playing at local weddings, parties, and restaurants in Colorado Springs.

DAVE PLAYING IN NASHVILLE, THE COVER OF HIS
ALBUM ON CONFIDANT CASSETTE, 1990

Dave has never married, but enjoys activities with many friends.

Noah's daughter, Debbie, is not only a Dental assistant, but is very talented in making high-end jewelry in her spare time. She lives near us in Chamblee. She has one daughter, Sarah, who is 31 and has two granddaughters, Bailee, who is seven and Marlee, who is three, which makes us "great-grands."

And while it would be great to have all of the children in Atlanta, they sure have picked some lovely places to live and for us to visit.

CHAPTER 24

Trouble

We were happy, the boys were well, and all seemed to be going as it should until we had been married five years when Jim started drinking. This was a shock as he and I never drank when we dated or at any time throughout our marriage. We just never had any interest.

Jim was an only child and his parents had helped us buy our first house and were quite involved with us. They were great babysitters and very appreciated. I just adored my Mother-in-law, Sara. I needed a mother, and she needed a daughter. I blamed my father-in-law for Jim's drinking. They would go hunting at the family farm in Cartersville, and Pop would have plenty of liquor. I didn't realize that Pop was an alcoholic and that there might be a genetic tendency toward alcoholism possible. Even though my own father was an alcoholic, I just didn't see it coming. Despite drinking heavily for the next thirteen years, Jim managed to attend Georgia Tech, keep a full-time job almost until the end, and graduate from Atlanta Law School. We had been married eighteen years and for the most part, the boys and I had worked around his alcoholism. In fact, he was very creative with ways to hide his bottles.

I had fired at least two babysitters because he or I blamed them. He continued to drink heavily, and the amount that he drank caught up with him. Even experiencing living with an alcoholic as I did with my parents and with Jim, I'm not 100% sure that I understand why they can't stop drinking, even if they want to. The changes that take place in their personalities can be unbelievable. The drinking affects everything and everyone in the family. I found empty liquor bottles in the toilet tanks, which kept them from flushing. I found them between the mattress and the bed springs. In a pair of his boots. Under his car seat. He would go so far as to replace a gallon jug of lemonade or water with vodka. It was such a waste. At the end he was in the hospital, and his liver and kidneys wouldn't forgive him anymore.

Jim had it all. He was a handsome, nice, smart man, and it was only when I thought that I was going crazy myself that I realized I couldn't live that way any longer. After I divorced him, Jim lived for one year and one week. He died at age 40. I am still mad at him, but I have since learned that it is a disease. It's just too hard to live with.

This was a sad time for all of us. I loved him still, but couldn't live that life anymore. I knew that I had to change my life or the situation was going to get me too. Depression had overtaken me at one point, and I got counseling, but it was hard to work. The boys were at home and going to high school. One morning I was so depressed that I wasn't sure I could get out of bed. I thought, "If I can just get one foot on the floor, maybe I can get up." That's when I decided to move forward with a divorce. After that whenever a friend talks to me about having the same problem and her husband won't go to AA, I tell her to run from the situation as fast as she can if she wants to have a happy life. Al-Anon, a support group for the families of alcoholics, helped me a lot, but unless the alcoholic goes for help, it can only have one ending.

CHAPTER 25

The Funeral and a Heavenly Visit

Jim's funeral was in the morning on a July 4th holiday weekend at Patterson's Funeral Home. Patterson's is an old Southern Institution in Atlanta, and everyone in our family was buried by Patterson's. Even with their tradition and our history, we had trouble getting flowers and scheduling the funeral. Also, they wouldn't dig a grave on a holiday, so getting the plot prepared at Arlington was delayed. Therefore, Jim was on view at the funeral home for four days. Since many were out of town for the holiday weekend, it gave them time to pay their respects.

I had explained to the boys, then young teenagers, we had to make it through the four days. When the guests started coming in for the service, the boys were instructed to greet them and ask if they would like to see their father. The first relative came in, and Dixon said, "Would you like to see what's left of my father?" Jim had lost weight, from 230 to 115 pounds in one year. What a sad thing for Dixon to say.

JIM PATRICK, AGE 38, IN 1974, 2 YEARS BEFORE HIS DEATH

We did make it through, and we came home after the funeral and I stretched out on my bed. The boys were in the carport fiddling with car parts. We were in a sort of shock.

I was lying there thinking about the time Jim and I met, our courtship and marriage, and our boys. I glanced over at the door to the bedroom, and there stood Jim, leaning against the door frame with his arms crossed in front, looking sixteen years old with a crew cut. He had on blue jeans and my favorite suede jacket of his. I used to love the way that suede jacket smelled. I looked down at myself to be sure that I was really awake. I *was* awake. He just smiled at me. He looked so well and happy. He didn't say anything or move toward me. I didn't experience any fear. I sincerely believe that he appeared to let me know that he was fine and happy. Then he faded away. I made the mistake of telling this to the doctor I worked for at the time, and he said that they called it "twilight sleep," not asleep but not awake. I told him that I was really sorry that I told him about it because I was *not* asleep. This was a true thing that happened to me.

CHAPTER 26

Transitional Time

After my divorce and Jim's death, I was single for about two and a half years. I had asked God to somehow let me know if He had another companion in mind for me. In fact, He says to ask for what you want, so I asked for everything: he must be kind, nice looking, and smart, and I even threw in he's not a sports fan. This was because Jim and his dad were Georgia Tech fans who got soused before every game. If Tech won, they were happy and drank together. If they lost, they drank even more and had reasons for Tech losing, such as "The sun was in their eyes," or "They weren't on their home turf," or something else. For years we attended not only home games but out of town games as well. It was a nightmare. I did forget to ask for a Christian man or one with money. Still, I got exactly what I needed...

A year after Jim died, my brother Larry, who had an executive search firm at the time, introduced me to a wonderful guy who was also just divorced. We went out every night for three months to drink coffee and talk. Larry thought that this guy was just as square as I was.

I remember when he came to my front door for our first date. I opened the door, and he looked so young I asked to see his driver's license! He finally said, "Well, are you going to let me in the house?" He had two boys and a girl, and I had two boys. He was Methodist, I was Methodist. I thought to myself, "Gee, this is so easy. I met the right one right away, and people said it would be so hard."

What I didn't realize was that this was my precious "transitional person." That's what counselors call them; they are the ones we talk it out with as we get ready to really date. I never thanked him for the conversations and relief from pain I felt. He also needed to talk and express his pain. Thank goodness we never crossed any line or boundaries that we would live to regret. We both realized that it is good advice not to get serious with someone until a year has passed. This is so true. People are too vulnerable to make sensible decisions right after the death of a spouse or a divorce. Also, there are many people who come into our lives for a season, but don't stay forever. I do think they come into our lives for a reason. This is true of friends of both genders. A counselor I worked for also said that it is important for us to claim our part of what went wrong in a relationship, and the time you take not rushing into another relationship is valuable for thinking that one out.

Anyway, around this time after the divorce, I felt that the boys and I needed to go on a little vacation. We were all traumatized with the events that had taken place. We decided to go non-stop to Washington, D.C. in my little orange Volkswagen. I don't even remember stopping for gas, but I'm sure we had to. It took us twelve hours. We stayed right in D.C. at the Iwo Jima Motel and went to the Smithsonian museums and the Arlington Cemetery where Dixon hid behind a bush and jumped out and scared me to death. When we were ready to go back to Atlanta, we realized the battery was dead in the VW. It was located under the back seat and was out of water. When we got back home, this lovely transitional man called me, and he broke off our relationship. He remains the only guy who ever dumped me.

CHAPTER 27

Mr. Right

One of my divorced friends, Shirley, who was beginning to consider dating, called me one night about the time I got home from working near Piedmont Hospital. I was dead tired, my hair was dirty, and I was looking forward to feeding myself and the boys and just flopping in front of the TV. Shirley wanted me to come to her house and "babysit" her while she met a new guy. She was being introduced by a neighbor to this guy, and she explained that the neighbor would be coming with her date. She was clear that the neighbor was *not* my date; he was simply accompanying her date. So after trying to beg off big time, Shirley said, "Have I been a good friend to you or what?" So I dragged myself over to her house that night and waited with her for her date.

Noah, who was called "Ed" at the time, walked into the room first. I was immediately attracted to him. The trouble was that he was Shirley's date, not mine.

He was already losing some hair on the top of his head, and he had permed—really—the medium brown hair on the sides of his head which made him look a little like Bozo the Clown. He had a handlebar mustache, and all in all was, I thought, probably an old interesting hippie. At 39, he was past the age, but nonetheless a really different kind of guy than one I thought I would be attracted to. Still, he was fascinating and so cute. His mustache hopped up and down when he talked. Later, he told me that he kept watching me out of the corner of his eye, and he thought my hair style was awful too. He said, "I knew there was a cute girl under that hairdo." I had spent a lot of money on what they called "the lamp cut" and having it was dyed red. I thought it was very modern.

About three weeks later, he called to ask me for a date, but I told him that I had to be sure that Shirley was through with him. I called Shirley, and she said they had a couple of dates, but neither of them was interested in continuing the relationship, so she gave me the go ahead. On our first date, he picked me up in his old Fiat, which had wires hanging down under the dashboard. I wondered if I could be accidently electrocuted. Noah's nickname for this old car was P.O.S., short for "piece of shit."

We went to a popular eating place in Buckhead called Good Old Days where they served flower pots with different foods baked in them. Afterwards, we went to the Chattahoochee

River bank near his apartment and threw rocks in the river. This is the truth. We realized right away that we were so very different, but also so attracted to each other. He had been married twice before and had a daughter. He was also fond of marijuana and eventually introduced me to it, which had its funny moments. This phase did not last very long. At one point we went to see a Cheech and Chong movie after smoking some pot. I was not used to it, and it really made me kind of numb. There was a long line at the movie, and he told me to stay there until he could get the tickets. I took his word for it and did not move an inch. People walked around me while I just stood exactly where he told me to.

I feel that sometimes opposites do attract. One of the Counselors that I worked for, Dr. Pete Hutchings, said that people with a fear of engulfment are attracted to people with a fear of abandonment. Is this the same thing as opposites attract? Maybe! I haven't really figured that out. Noah rounded up my square corners, and I squared up his round ones. He was the most romantic guy that I ever dated, and the only one that my boys really liked. I think children have a certain feel for who would be right for their mamas. The boys had nicknames for the others like "Stretch Armstrong" or "The Milk Man."

We married at the Dunwoody United Methodist Church Chapel on May 12, 1979. Rev. Linda Jones officiated. My mother's family was so conservative that they weren't used to a woman being a minister. They thought Linda was going to sing! Noah's mother was 45 minutes late to the wedding "because I just couldn't get ready," and Noah is still mad at her even though she died some time ago! After the wedding, we had a reception at the house on Spalding Drive, and after that, we took off for our honeymoon on the Chattanooga Choo Choo in one of their train cars.

Dunwoody United Methodist Church, May 12, 1979

Mr. and Mrs. Noah Byrd at breakfast on the morning after

their honeymoon at the Chattanooga Choo Choo

Today Noah and I are very much alike in our thinking and values. With a little luck, that's what 36 years together will do. He was the man I had asked God to show me. And we are both in our late seventies, still so in love. Still loving to be with each other more than doing anything else. Life is good. Childhood memories are beginning to fade. I say "Thank you, God" many times in my mind and sometimes out loud.

We repeated our vows in the Roswell United Methodist Church Chapel on our 15th anniversary. Dave came to visit from Nashville and played his guitar at the service, and we had a reception for our Sunday School Class.

I was understandably jealous of both of Noah's ex-wives. One is a lovely blond who was his childhood sweetheart and the mother of his daughter, Debbie. The other was a diminutive brunette who had lived with him for three years before their marriage, which lasted four more years. He had told me that "she was a wild one," and they had had some wild and crazy times together. Wife #1, Barbara, had married again, and she and Noah were good friends, so she and her husband Bob were invited to our wedding. It took longer for me to get to know Wife #2. When the first grandchild, Sarah, was born to Noah's daughter, I thought to myself, "this little baby girl can have several grandparents, not just two." After that, we started sharing holidays and birthdays, sicknesses, ups and downs with all the kids, loss of parents, and generally being an extended family. We call ourselves "The Wives Club." We keep in close touch, and we have faced some big things together. Noah's daughter has survived kidney cancer and a horrendous car accident. Wife #1 has had breast cancer surgery and two hip surgeries. Wife #2 had an undiagnosed blood disorder, and unfortunately had a stroke and passed away in April of 2015 as I was writing this memoir. Since my boys both live out west and we don't see them a lot, together we have an extended family, now with three grandchildren and two great grandchildren.

Dixon, Deb, Mamie, us, Dave, wedding day at Dunwoody UMC

"The Wives Club" L-R Barbara Farmer #1,
Dusty Foster #2, Lynne Byrd #3, 2013

CHAPTER 28

Life on Spalding Drive with the Crew

After we married, I asked Noah if he minded moving in with the boys and me on Spalding so that they could finish North Springs High School. Then, I explained, we could sell the house and find something that the two of us had chosen. But we stayed there twenty more years together.

For the time all of us lived together, I painted a mailbox with all of us on it: The two dachshunds, the two boys, one girl and the two of us. I thought it was really cute. The mailman called on me after I put it up and told me that the kids at North Springs High School would knock it down. First, if they won a ball game, and secondly, if they lost a ball game. So we put screws in the bottom very lightly to hold it on the post, and when they would knock it off, it would just fly off and land in the pine straw! Step-daughter Debbie only lived with us for a little while until she went into the Air Force, where she was trained to be a Dental Assistant, and served in Air Force Bases in the Azores and in the United States in Michigan.

OUR MAILBOX ON SPALDING DRIVE, SHOWING OUR ENTIRE NEW FAMILY

My memories of the boys' teenage years are good ones. The boys both had bicycles and motorcycles, and they had a course in our yard which wore a groove in the dirt. They also had a cool tree house in the front yard with a ladder and rope to open and close the door for privacy. I'm not sure our neighbors were too fond of all of this going on, but they never complained. The yard was wooded enough and large enough to accommodate all of this. They also were both mechanical, and they loved to take their bikes—or anything—apart and put them back together just for the heck of it.

The four of us were good friends, and Dixon says now that he has two daughters himself, that there was "about the right amount of discipline." The best part of being a parent, if you are lucky, is watching your kids become adults who make good decisions. However, if I had it all to do over again, I would do some things differently. I would wait until I was old enough to have some sense before starting a family. Nineteen was way too young, and God looked after me in my stupidity when dealing with new babies. I would try to figure out a way to stay home with my babies. And I would read to them more. I once saw a wall plaque that read, "Richer than me you will never be.....I had a mother who read to me."

After both boys had graduated from high school, Noah and I made our own memories and savored them.

CHAPTER 29

The Other Woman

Lest you think that our marriage has always been perfect, I want to share a time with you when it was not so perfect. It was 1986, and we were both real estate agents. All of a sudden on a Monday in October, the interest rates on home mortgages jumped by 2%. This made most of our real estate contracts null and void, because our buyers were unable to afford the higher payments. The real estate agents in our office were all sitting around staring into space saying, "It just can't be true."

House values went down and potential customers fell away. Everybody buttoned up to ride out this period. Since both of us were in real estate, we said to each other, "What are we going to do?" Our money-making prospects were not looking good; in fact, they were terrible. So, I suggested that for a while I would go back to medical transcription. It was easy for me to find a job because medical transcription is needed whether the stock market or house sales are good or not, and I had hospital experience.

So for a year, I typed all day long as fast as I could, because we were paid 2 cents a line. This is a lot like working in a sweat shop, except instead of sewing, we were typing. The company I worked for was in the basement of a medical building, and we had about thirty typists who did the same thing I did. We all had our special accounts. For instance, on Mondays I had an eye surgeon who mostly removed cataracts. Tuesday, it might be a mixture of gallbladders and other stomach surgery. Wednesday it might be a psychiatrist who was dictating long distance from a prison or mental hospital. Thursday could be all histories and physicals for pre-ops. It did have its benefits though. I would say to myself, "Today I will do cataracts." Then I would envision the gurneys lined up outside the operating room, waiting for my services.

I especially enjoyed one of my clients who was a Hispanic Psychiatrist, dictating from the Federal Prison in Atlanta. His patients were all Cubans who had been detained as a result of the Mariel boatlift in 1980 during the Jimmy Carter administration. I enjoyed overcoming his accent and was interested in the various tattoos the prisoners had. Most of them had a tattoo of their mother.

However, I was working my buns off and Noah was not. He was in love with the early version of the computer, a Commodore 64, and while he was certainly teaching himself a usable skill for later, it was making me madder and madder to come home and find that nothing was done: no dinner, no housework, and especially, no time for me. Around this same time, I was taking a Creative Writing class after work at Georgia State, and I wrote a short story featuring this same problem, and what happened.

The Other Woman

Anne hated her husband's computer. She had no interest in this or any similar technology. She didn't understand what the attraction was. She opened her eyes and looked at the clock: 5:00 a.m. He was already at it. Working away on that hateful bitch machine. A narrow band of light shone brightly under the door. The light was coming from his computer room, a tiny unfriendly tomb-like place which used to be their smallest bedroom.

Damn, she thought. Why, on a Saturday morning, would Ed leave her and their warm cozy bed to work in that freezing little place? What could be so important that it had to be done before the sun came up? She clenched her teeth, moaned and rolled over.

Anne had met Ed at the home of a girlfriend ten years ago. Marcia was another divorcee who threw wonderful parties for all of her single friends, hoping to be a cupid, either for herself or for them. Anne had reluctantly gone to one of the parties. She really hadn't wanted to go…she was so tired and had worked all day and her hair could use a nice soapy washing and conditioning. But Ed had been there. She had been fascinated with him from the beginning. He was so unlike her. He was a daredevil, a risk taker. Anne called him "round," and she felt like she was "square." She had never known anyone quite like Ed. He was an adorable, slightly balding chap; a left-over sixties hippie in a forty year old body. He had swept Anne off her feet with his free-spirited gentle ways and his constant attention. He had introduced Anne to things she had never experienced. Art films. White water canoeing. Little theatre. Even some marijuana. They laughed all the time. He had been married twice before, but he had never had a real wedding, so after he popped the question and she said "yes," Anne had worn a white bridal gown and had a real wedding, so that he might have his first bride. It had been so much fun! Theirs had been the perfect marriage—or almost—for ten whole years. Until the computer came into their lives. This marriage, Anne felt, was her reward for surviving an unhappy childhood and eighteen years with her first husband, who had made her life miserable and managed to drink himself to death at age 40. Everyone thought that Anne and Ed were perfect for each other, even her own two teenaged boys. "How did you meet?" people would ask. She had never expected the honeymoon to last forever...but it had...for ten years...until the computer came along. He was in a family business with his father and brother and decided that he couldn't do without one.

Only one short year ago, Saturday morning would have been so different. She and Ed would have stayed in bed and snuggled until about 9 o'clock or so. Then maybe they would go to the Hickory House for breakfast: ham, eggs, and red eye gravy. Then the anticipation of something special for the rest of the weekend. He was so clever coming up with special ideas—maybe an auction or a festival in the mountains. She never knew what the weekend might hold. Now, he spent day after day in the house with that little steel box who had taken on all of the aspects of another woman. Ed spent so much time fiddling with it, forgetting to eat, losing weight. Irritable all the time. She went to work and school and out with friends, but he wanted to stay home in the little office... with *her*. Friends took valuable time away from his computer. Anne fell back to sleep listening to the soft sounds of his laser printer...*whirr...whirr...whirr...*

Anne was determined that this Saturday, Ed would not spend the day with his computer. This Saturday would be different. She got up, washed her face, took off her nightgown and walked naked into the office. She saw Ed looking at the computer with a look she had seen many times, a look meant for her—a loving look. She decided against a direct reprimand. No need to start a fight first thing. "Good morning!" Anne said. She kissed her husband on the shiny top of his head, a place she called "the sweet spot."

He was wearing his ratty white chenille bathrobe with the "E" on the pocket, hunched over the keyboard in an intimate way, his warm fingers punching on the keys in a steady, familiar rhythm. He paused briefly and looked up at her.

"Hi pussycat...*Well*! What have we here? Aren't you something else! Aren't you afraid the joggers will see you through the window? Why don't you just dance around and sing, "Hi, Neighbor!" Ed was jovial enough, but his blue eyes were bloodshot, and he had more than the beginnings of a beard.

Anne treated him to her best smile, and she tried a centerfold pose. "Breakfast can be ready in a jiffy. Those great bagels you like so much. I got the ones with the garlic salt. How about it?"

Ed rubbed his eyes and stretched. "No...not hungry, hon,... she has this glitch in the program and...you go ahead...I don't want anything."

Outside, storm clouds were gathering. Anne loved storms. She always felt sexy during a storm. Once, lightening had hit the computer and the modem—whatever in Hell that was—and it had blown up. Ed was devastated and had blamed himself.

"She's down!" he croaked. "I should have backed her up. I should have unplugged her!" And on and on.

Anne had had him to herself for three days while the part was on order, but he had paced around the little room like a lost soul most of the time, complaining. Things were not the same as they had once been, of course, but at least he wasn't able to spend all of his time on the computer. They had watched TV together, and he had even fixed a surprise dinner one night for her.

Anne crossed the hall into the small bathroom. On the sink were piles of computer magazines and brochures. These people really knew how to hook you. Anne wondered if she would have felt differently if they had been Playboy magazines. No, it would have felt the same. She stared in the mirror and pushed at her hair. Attractive enough, she thought. Not bad at all. Tonight, she mused, I will seduce him away from that home wrecker. I want my husband back.

The doorbell rang, and Anne threw on her housecoat and ran down the stairs. She opened the door and saw one of Ed's computer nerd groupies, Dennis.

Dennis was always showing up at the wrong time. Dennis was not very bright and absolutely idolized Ed. He had purchased a computer with Ed's help and was always either calling or bugging them to death getting help trying to operate the damn thing. "Hello, Dennis. What is it this time?"

Dennis shoved past Anne and raced up the stairs to the computer room. He was not one for small talk. He wanted to get right to the source: Ed.

Anne spent the morning cleaning house and fuming to herself about Dennis being upstairs with her husband and the computer. What was so interesting about "software" and "bytes" and "downloading?" She had to admit that she was jealous of Ed, the computer, and his nerdy friends.

She decided to seduce him. She knew what he liked. She herself was turned on by candlelit dinners and wine and sweet words…but Ed, yes, she knew what he liked. He had given her a red sequined bikini outfit from Frederick's on her 40th birthday. She had been so surprised. She thought she looked like a Ruben's painting in it. Ed, on the other hand, thought she looked wonderful. He had taken pictures of her stretched out on the bed in it. She hadn't put it on in a long, long time. Tonight was definitely the night.

It made no sense to be jealous of a machine. And to feel like it was a woman. But it was. And the machine knew that she knew. She felt negative vibrations every time she went anywhere near it. She felt that the computer was drawing Ed toward itself while pushing her away. Her eyes fell back to the computer magazines. Pieces of toilet paper were stuffed between the pages where Ed had marked equipment that he wanted to buy. She flipped to a particularly large bulge and found an invoice for $234.00 for a fancy color program and other supplies.

She crossed the hall into the computer room and put the bill directly in front of his face.

"Did you buy this stuff, Ed?"

"Oh, no, hon," Ed blinked. "It's for Les Chessman in our computer club. I told him I would pick it up for him."

Dennis, the Nerd, looked up at Anne as though she were an invading foreigner. What a creepy little guy.

"And I suppose you also put it on our Visa?" Anne hated sounding like a fishwife, but she knew he was lying. He never used to lie, and they never used to fight. He had bought something new for the computer, and he was lying about it. Totally frustrated, lips pressed together hard, she leaned over and switched off the computer. A sharp shock ran up Anne's arm.

Ed jumped up, knocking over his chair, and screamed, "Don't you ever, EVER, do that again! You have to exit her properly!"

Anne stalked out. Well, she thought, like I give three rows of rat shit. She then thought to herself that Dennis was getting a good picture of married life when you are nuts about a dumb computer. But, on the other hand, who in the world would marry *Dennis*? Nobody. It would never be a problem!

Anne grabbed her purse and got in the car. Nothing to do but go shopping. Shopping always calmed her down. She had often thought there was a "shopping gene" in her family, a dominant gene transmitted to all of the females. This gene was like a white blood cell fighting infection. The shopping gene warded off depression and despair. A good gene. A useful gene.

A day in the mall had worn off her anger at Ed, and she looked forward to her seduction that night. Driving home she mentally picked out her perfume—he loved Modern Muse by Estee Lauder. And she would wear jewelry too. And really red lipstick. Her mind scavenged the cupboard for some wine. She found some nice steaks at the local Publix…and of course, the Pink Floyd tape. Yes, this would really be fun. And Ed would wonder why it had been so long. The anticipation was almost too great to bear.

Ed was where she had left him. Anne wondered how often he got a drink of water and when he went to the bathroom. He was still in his chenille robe, hunched over his beloved machine. Dennis, thankfully, was gone. She really needed to get that robe off and get it washed. How depressing. He used to be so particular about what he wore…now nothing seemed to matter but doing something on that computer.

It had not stormed after all, but rain was softly falling and it was getting dark outside. Anne stood quietly at the door watching Ed's face. She walked around the side of his desk so that she could see the screen. The new program he had bought for the computer was in brilliant color, really beautiful color. She had a fleeting vision of earrings hanging off the computer and a smart little hat sitting on the top of its head. Waves of dislike seemed to be directed at her from the machine. The buttons were arranged on the keyboard in such a way that it seemed to be frowning at Anne. I must be crazy, she thought.

Ed's eyes were dreamily gazing into the screen. He had not heard her come in, and he was murmuring in a low voice, "Now come on baby. Don't crash. Do this for me…"

Anne imagined she saw the screen brighten up in response. These two were quite a pair. Ed looked sick and pale, like a patient in an institution who never saw the sun. Anne tried to remember how long it had been since he had left the house. She couldn't remember. Days. Quite a few days.

She slid her arm around him and hugged him from behind.

"Honey," she said, "How would you like an old fashioned orgy tonight? And maybe a steak and Pink Floyd?" Anne was slightly repulsed by his body odor.

Ed sort of shook her off, but said, "Great, great…I'll just work along here until dinner's ready. Yeah…you just call me…"

Ed had not even looked up. She could have been anyone. Anyone could have just walked right into their house and hugged Ed and stolen everything. He wouldn't have noticed. He wouldn't have known. A disgusted feeling flooded Anne which was new to her. The feeling was a red and blue rage made of helplessness and anger. But mostly of fear. If something didn't happen to break his fascination with this machine, it was possible that she could lose Ed for good…maybe she had already lost him. Maybe he was going crazy.

It was worth a try. Anne hoped she could lure him away from the little office at least for the evening. It could be a turning point. She took out the steaks and lit the grill. Found the wine hiding behind those strawberry preserves her mother-in-law kept sending over. Nouveau Beaujolais. His very favorite. Her spirits lifted a little. It was raining a little harder outside now. A few distant sounds of thunder. Good! From downstairs she could hear the steady whirr of the printer. She went to her chest-of-drawers and pulled out the teeny weeny little bikini outfit. My God, Anne thought, this thing would hardly fit a Barbie Doll!

She put it on and rummaged in her purses until she found the lipstick. Her stomach bulged over the shiny fabric. But Ed would love it! The perfect whore, she thought, I'll be the perfect whore. A flash of lightening outside. Another clap of thunder. She found the Pink Floyd tape in the bottom of the tape drawer and rammed it in the CD player. *Dark Side of the Moon.* Ed had wired the house last Christmas and put speakers in every room. Pink Floyd drifted all over. She knew that Ed could hear it in the computer room too. Maybe it would get him in the mood. Pink Floyd was theirs. Before that computer, there was Pink Floyd. Anne tiptoed downstairs to finish dinner. No need to bother him until everything was ready. Wasn't she a sight in this outfit?! What if their preacher, Rev. Smith, were to call on them now? Anne Dawson, teacher of the ten year old Sunday School class, in a sequined bikini. I'd love to see his little fat face when he gets a load of me, she thought.

Anne turned off all the lights and lit the candles. She started the tape over on the first side and glanced round to be sure everything was perfect. It was. The storm was getting worse. The thunder was closer…and louder…she started up the steps to the computer room. Ed had been sitting there the whole day. No breakfast. No lunch. A visit from Dennis, the computer nerd. This was it. She was going to get her hands on that husband of hers and make him remember how good Saturday nights used to be. She stepped inside the office, and Ed looked up.

He looked genuinely surprised this time. "Well….well….well…"

She carefully slid along the wall of the office, sucking her stomach in and trying to look as much like a femme fatale as possible.

"Ed, I want you, and I want you now…I miss you, and I'm sick of sharing you with that computer. What—?" She took a breath. "—do *you* want?"

"God, Anne. You women are crazy. All I'm doing is trying to figure out this program."

"What do you want, Ed?" A tear trickled from her right eye, and she was trying hard to be calm.

Ed got up and crossed over to her and put his arms gently around her. "Have I really ignored you that much? Give me two more hours, pussycat, and I'll be finished. I promise."

Anne shook her head and hugged him hard. "No, Ed. Now. I've got a wonderful evening planned. It's got to be now. We have steaks. We have wine. We have Pink Floyd. Let the computer wait. Not me."

Ed stepped away from her and his chin tilted up in the air just a little. "I said two hours. I'll be all done in two hours."

Anne packed her overnight bag and put her favorite jewelry in the side pocket. She took off the red sequined outfit and put it in the bathroom trash can. She felt embarrassed. Men are so different, she thought. I don't understand. I don't even want to understand. I don't even care anymore. Who needs this? Who can compete with a machine?

She wasn't careful to be particularly quiet as she stumbled down the stairs, her bag bumping along. Pink Floyd insistently filled the air. She passed through the kitchen, but didn't even glance at the table which had been set for such a wonderful evening. Best china, candles lit. Out on the patio, the grill was fiery red, waiting for steaks which would not be cooked tonight, steaks which would not be eaten by lovers.

The windshield wipers were in perfect rhythm with the car radio as Anne pulled out of the driveway. The song on the radio was *Feelings*.

"Ten wonderful years," Anne said aloud. "A lot of people don't even get that."

* * *

This is a true story. The "Ed" in the story is my husband, and "Anne" is me, but I never left that night. Thank goodness he saw the error of his ways and took me up on my kind offer that Saturday night. It was a critical time. He still loves the computer and is a whiz on it. He helps his friends with their problems and uses it in real estate. I swear I think he could get it to make coffee. But he understood how I felt, which is all that mattered.

CHAPTER 30

The "Not a Christian" Thing

In our marriage, the "not a Christian" thing was more of a problem than I had anticipated. I was sure that after we were married, he would automatically become a Christian. But it didn't happen that way. After about two years of my putting him on a pedestal and worshipping him, I missed going to church. He looked at me and said, "I wondered how long it would last before you missed your people." So, to make a really long story short, we visited all kinds of churches and all kinds of denominations. He had no problem getting up and getting dressed and going with me, but he just never felt anything special at church.

This lasted for twelve long years! No kidding.

So one Sunday, I said, "Look Honey, you and I have a great marriage. Just stay home and read the paper, and I'll go to church by myself."

He gave me a look I had not seen on his face before and said, "If you give up on me, God is going to be really pissed at you.

So, God *was* drawing him in, and I didn't even know it.

Shortly after this, the Christmas season was in full swing, and we both liked to sing, so we went to Roswell Methodist Church in Roswell, Georgia to hear their Christmas program, which was terrific. We decided then to visit that church more, and we ended up joining the choir and a Sunday school class.

A few more months passed, and we were invited to go on a Christian weekend called "The Walk to Emmaus." The men go first to the camp, and the next weekend the wives go. So, Noah found Christ on his weekend and told me, "We have work to do!"

NOAH AT ROSWELL METHODIST CHURCH, 1992

This program is called by different names in different denominations, but offers the same weekend. After Noah's walk, we invited Christ into our marriage as the third person, and He has remained there for us in all of our decisions, problems, and blessings. We have been singing in choirs for about twenty-five plus years. I have enjoyed this very much, but my voice isn't what it used to be, so I dropped out and have become a choir groupie and #1 fan.

During the first part of our marriage, "Ed" had worked with his family in a high-end family upholstery business in Roswell. This was followed by Noah's desire to get his hairdresser's license, which he did. For about five years he managed a beauty salon until he developed pain in both shoulders, mainly from rolling perms. Today, the hairdressers like to use a hot iron or blow out the hair. When he went to beauty school, the time came when he had to leave the plastic dummies with wigs and work on a real person, so he used me for a guinea pig. At different times I was a blond, a redhead, and one time I had almost no hair as I watched it go down the drain.

He felt that his name, "Ed", was not a good name for a hairdresser. "Mr. Ed sounds like a friggin' horse," he said, referring to the talking horse on the 1960s television show *Mr. Ed*. So, he switched his name to "Mr. Noah," his middle name, a much classier sound. All of his friends and family had to do a switcheroo and call him Noah from that point on. It was very hard for us to call him Noah, but his mother said, "If I can do it, anybody can." And she was right.

CHAPTER 31

A New Career for Us

Noah's Dad, who started the family upholstery business years before, was not well and was getting close to retirement. Ralph, Noah's brother, was also thinking about doing something new. About the same time, I was thinking about leaving the Administration Department of St. Joseph's Hospital, especially if Noah and I could figure out something to do together. The three of us sat down to discuss it, and our list of things that our new job must include (1) we could be together most of the time; (2) every day would be a new experience and would be a chance to meet new people; and (3) hopefully we could make money! Real Estate is what we decided we would do.

So we enrolled in a real estate course through DeKalb College at night, spent a whole quarter really learning it well, and took our real estate exams and passed them. The three of us went to work for Century 21 in 1986. We refinanced our house and withdrew $15,000 to tide us over until we could make a sale. It turned out that all of us were pretty good at real estate, and we enjoyed it. The company we picked was Century 21 in a great location in Roswell where we were fortunate to get customers from desk duty and our broker Lynn Williams.

The hardest part of being a real estate agent for me was finding my way around. This was before GPS, and I was never very good at directions or map reading. So, I would preview each and every house that I planned to show the day before and do such things like meet the pets and learn where the lights and the closets were. I could write a book on the experiences that we and our fellow real estate agents had. I'm not going to, but somebody should. Customers would sometimes say, "This is so much fun looking at houses. I'd like to be a real estate agent!" So I would gently tell them that I would be glad to treat them to lunch if they ever seriously wanted to be an agent, and I would tell them all of the good things about it and all of the bad too. It is a consuming way to work—you must be ready every day and at all hours to show or list a house, or write a contract. You must be self-motivated and generally be able to work with all types of people. And you must get used to having your heart broken occasionally.

Noah, his brother Ralph, and I were all in the "Million Dollar Club," and Noah and I both got our Broker's License. We opened Byrd Realty, Inc., and enjoyed being our own boss for 29 years. Noah is still the best agent I know. He is scrupulously honest, good at math, and an absolute whiz at the

CENTURY 21, ROSWELL, "TOP TEAM BYRD" OF

RALPH, NOAH, AND LYNNE BYRD, 1986

computer, which is where real estate has gone with its forms and contracts, as well as as researching available properties.

Well, I said I wouldn't write a book, but here's a few of our real estate stories:

Like me, Noah also liked to preview homes before showing them, and he was walking around one house, memorizing the details, when he looked into the back yard and saw a big gray dog. He loves animals and liked to make friends with them so they would know him when he returned with his clients. He whistled to the dog and the closer the dog got, the more Noah realized that he was a big gray pig…who wanted to be petted! Of course, Noah *did* pet him and made friends, then even greeted him the next day when he showed the property.

Still another time, Noah had worked with a delightful couple moving to Atlanta from out west. They found the perfect house and were so looking forward to the move. On moving day, along with their furniture and clothing, the couple had included their fancy sports car. Straps were attached to the car to keep it stabilized while moving. A strap on the car's tire had obviously started rubbing against the tire and eventually it caught on fire. The whole van burned up with everything they had, including their car! They moved into their lovely new home and slept on air mattresses on the floor. We took them food and a cooler of assorted drinks. They took this so calmly, I'm sure they must have been in shock.

My real estate friend Betty Pittard Long once had a customer who was anxious to see a particular house, and it had to be seen that day. Betty pulled up to the house with her customers, and through the glass sidelights of the house, Betty saw a long snake bumping against the glass. This of course freaked out the customers. So, she opened the lockbox, grabbed a shovel, opened the door, killed the snake, and showed the house. And yes, it's true—the snake was the household pet. And the clients bought the house!

Noah and I had an unusually rewarding sale to a celebrity. The unique home was situated on a large property and was filled with fine art and antiques. It was Christmastime, and the owners had requested no showings during the week. Then I had a call from an agent who wanted me to show the house to her celebrity customers on Christmas Eve! After much explanation, the owners obliged, and I forewarned the potential customers we would be interrupting a family occasion, so we would just stroll through the house and grounds, and if interested, we could come back in a few days.

At 7 pm on Christmas Eve, the real estate agent and her customers met me at the bottom of the long driveway where we began a slow approach to a house which was stunningly lit for the holiday. When the owner answered the doorbell, the door opened to a scene of a perfect family: grandma in a rocking chair with her hair in a bun, beautiful children and grandchildren, a roaring fire in a huge fireplace with a big dog lying next to it. We all froze in the entryway for a moment to take in this tableau.

The customers loved the house, and we met again the day after Christmas for another showing. While chatting at the dining room table, they admitted that not only did they love the house, but they wanted everything in it! The owners agreed to sell the house and about 75% of the contents to the couple. Noah made hundreds of pictures of the art work and furniture in order to determine what was to stay and what the owners would sell. It was an intensive transaction!

Noah and I were invited to the clients' wedding, and we became fast friends with their real estate agent and other friends. Truly a happy ending!

As a realtor, you follow your leads and take help whenever it comes to make a sale. The Saints can even be of assistance!

When we first listed one house, the seller asked us to bury a statue of St. Joseph so the house would sell. This was the first time we had the request. We looked at each other and asked her to explain exactly what that meant. "Well," she said, "you get a statue of St. Joseph, the Carpenter, and bury him in our yard with the face toward the street. Then each morning, you and I say a prayer to St. Joseph, and when the house sells, we will dig him up, and I will take him with us to my new house." So, I went to the monastery on Riverside Drive near where we lived, and I found the little gift shop right outside the monastery. This was all new to me, so I walked in and said sheepishly, "I'm looking for a gift for a friend. I thought perhaps a statue of St. Joseph?" And she quickly replied, "Oh. Real estate agent?" "Uh, yeah." She then pulled out a *crate* of St. Joseph statues, and I bought one. So this wasn't anything new to her.

After Noah secured a contract on the house, Noah and I were together when we attended the inspection. This can be quite a lengthy process, and we were walking around the house with the buyers, making small talk. Noah turns to the buyers

and says, "You won't believe how we sold this house! We buried a statue of St. Joseph." And at that, the buyers turned to us and said, "How do you think we sold our house in Detroit?"

I was taking a folklore course at Georgia State University at the time this happened, and I reported this to my professor, Dr. Burrison, who asked me to do a paper on Real Estate Folklore. I did, and had a wonderful time documenting many interesting things that builders and buyers do, and customs of people who move to Atlanta from other countries. *Vive la différence!*

CHAPTER 32

My Bucket List

Getting married so young, it had always been a dream of mine to go back to school, so I made my Bucket List around 1982. I shared it with my book club, the Bella Literati Book Club, one night when we were doing our famous—but not always popular with everyone—"Twenty Questions." This little exercise we did at least three times during the 29 years we have been together. One of the questions was "What would you like to accomplish in the years to come?" I had thought and thought about going back to school to finish college, but at this point, I was 42. So, I asked myself, "Could I possibly be able to go to the local community college and do real estate at the same time? Will the younger students accept me? How will I get through the math?" I was just as afraid of going back to school after such a long time as any eighteen year old would be going to college for the first time. I had a year's worth of credits from the University of Georgia, but when I was a freshman at Georgia, I was in love and just wanted to get my one year over with and marry Jim, so my grades didn't reflect my best effort. Most of the Bellas had finished college and thought it was a great idea. They agreed, "You go for it, girl!" Noah also encouraged me, although he had gone into the Air Force at an early age and had only taken a few college courses.

So with some fear and trepidation I wrote down "Get Associate Degree" on my Bucket List as #1. I had my grades transferred to a two year community college near me, and I took the plunge, surprising myself how much I loved going to school. The younger students—most were around 18, fresh from high school—treated me the same way they treated each other. I loved them! Since Noah and I were still working in real estate and I was going to school at night, it took a while to get through just the two year program. In fact, it took four years. I found that I loved going to school just about more than anything, and I surprised myself by doing very well, except in math, my nemesis!

My experience with the one required math course was a combination of sweating bullets and praying that somehow, someway I would be able to make it through. It seemed to be a good idea to go ahead and take math and French, my foreign language, first and get them over with. The math course was a combination of basic algebra, geometry, and metric system material. My professor was just the best. From Brooklyn, he was an excellent teacher, but this didn't do much for my right-sided brain self. I went to him in desperation and asked, "Can I write a research paper on math perhaps?" Sadly, he said, "Oh, Lynne, I'm so sorry, but you just have to pass this test all by yourself."

I hate to admit it, but in jest, Noah said, "You have my permission to give him a blow job if he will pass you in math." He knew how awful I was in math, but he was kidding…I hope…

The day of the final test came, and the professor had allowed us to have a regular calculator as well as a metric calculator. I had also made a stack of index cards with permission, but unfortunately with a red felt-tip pen, to help me remember different formulas and equations. By the end of the final test, I had a terrible headache and my hands were perspiring with red ink all over them. I felt like fainting and stopped at the water cooler and then rested before making my way home. A couple of weeks later, my grades came in the mail. When Noah picked me up at school, he had cut out a piece of paper to fit the car window, and it said in one huge letter, "B". So I had made it through. Praise God and the Entire Heavenly Host. Amen!

After graduating with my Associate's Degree, it was about time for the Bellas to have another twenty questions meeting. This time, I wondered if it would be possible to go ahead and finish my undergraduate at Georgia State and earn my B.A. I got a printed catalogue and decided that Anthropology would be a really interesting degree since I had always loved antiques, studying other cultures, and preservation of historical properties. Again, I asked my book club buddies if this seemed like something I could do. After all, it was one thing to go to a community college and quite another to go to downtown Atlanta to a huge University. Again, all of those precious friends said, "You go, girl!" but this time with a little more conviction. So, I wrote down on my Bucket List, "#2. Get Undergraduate B.A. in Anthropology." I was able to stay in real estate since I had my husband/partner Noah, and go to school simultaneously to get my degree.

I loved every minute of it. This time, the students were very diverse from all countries and many cultures that I had never had any contact with. I was older than all of the students *and* all of my professors, which was funny, but they were so sweet to me and included me in everything. Once a bunch of the young ones asked me, "Hey Lynne, do you want to stay up all night and study for the final with us?" I said, "Hell no! I can't stay up all night! Anyway, I've already studied. I'm ready for the final."

It had been my way while going to school to take tons of notes on three-holed paper in class, which was a good thing as laptops weren't on the market in 1982. I knew how to take shorthand and developed even more short-cuts so I could go faster, like I stopped crossing the t's and dotting the i's. If someone was out and was really sick or had a good excuse, I would share my notes with them. If they were just goofing off, I wasn't so generous. Our Anthropology group was the greatest. My mentor was Dr. Valerie Fennell, who gave me an incentive to continue on with my education. She became a dear friend and mentor.

Dr. Fennell also gave me an appreciation of women in other cultures and taught a class called "Women in Cross Cultural Perspective." We had been assigned a book which included a lesbian couple. This was just one of the things I was not familiar with as I had never met a lesbian couple. So, in front of all of our class, she asked me what I thought a lesbian couple did, and I replied, "Well, I think they go to bed together naked." Being the oldest one in the class did not serve me well that day, and Dr. Fennell explained that homophobia was a big problem in America. I was honestly clueless. I then said, "Does that mean that I am a "homophobia?" I didn't even know the correct term, which was "homophobic." The same thing was true when a fellow student made a talk about "STDs." I had no idea what that stood for, which was "Sexually Transmitted Diseases."

Aside from Dr. Fennell, my favorite teacher was Dr. Blakely, who taught Forensic Anthropology, a darling man who loved to teach, and unfortunately died of cancer a couple of years after my graduation. Dr. Blakely would describe an early genus of mankind such as Australopithecus Woman nicknamed "Lucy," and he would demonstrate how she walked by limping around the classroom and flopping his arms. We all adored him. At the beginning of the class, he explained that the different skulls and bones we would get to use were fragile. He said, "Accidents happen, and if you should accidently chip or drop one, just come and tell me. I have glue." I am ashamed to say that the Neanderthal skull and the Australopithecus skull were side by side, and I slammed them into one another not being careful enough, causing a fracture in one of the skulls. Of course I immediately told him about it but felt very bad. So I did finish my B.A., scratched off #2 on the Bucket List, and wanted so much to try for a Master's.

Noah encouraged me to just go ahead and finish my Master's in Historic Preservation, but I wasn't sure that our marriage could survive a Master's program at that point with so much time devoted to study. Again, the Bellas said, "Of course you can!" And Noah agreed. So I put "Get Graduate Degree" on my Bucket List as #3.

DR. JOHN BURRISON, FOLK LIFE PROFESSOR

I was about as happy as a pig in mud at this time. To put the icing on the cake, I was able to do a two-year internship at The Atlanta History Center working on my minor in Folklore. They paid part of my tuition, and the school covered most of the rest. In fact, Noah and I figured that my entire Master's program cost about $1,500. My mentor, and head of the Folk life program, was Dr. John Burrison. He was unable to drive because of an eye problem, and so, whoever his intern was at the time got to drive him around to interview and document amazing people, like the Hewell folk potters of North Georgia, the wood basket makers of South Georgia, a lace maker, Carolina wood carvers, quilters, and Hmong basket weavers from Vietnam who had immigrated to Atlanta. What a privilege to be a part of a permanent folklore exhibit which is still there. An opportunity also came my way when Noah and I went to England. Dr. Burrison asked me to go to Herstmonceaux, in the Southern part of England where garden trugs (baskets) are made the same way they have been for over 100 years. My assignment was to interview the owner and the trug makers, take slides, and come back with a presentation. Noah and I spent a day there. The trug makers were all older artists, hand splitting the wood from old cricket bats, and then soaking them in water and steaming them in an ancient brick furnace to bend them into shape. This project was a guaranteed "A."

LYNNE'S GRADUATION DAY AND 55TH BIRTHDAY, JUNE 25, 1996,
WITH SON DAVID AND GRANDDAUGHTERS SAMANTHA, BRENDA, AND SARAH

Graduating on my 55th birthday was bittersweet. My three granddaughters were there, and I promised them that "If Mimi can do it, you can too." Seeing a dream come true made me so thankful and so happy. I really didn't want to leave.

Having crossed off #1, #2, and #3, it was time again to look at the Bucket List. I let my mind just go anywhere it wanted to, considered our family's resources, and thought about hundreds of things I wanted to still do. I said out loud to myself, "I want to run The Fourth of July Peachtree Road

Race in Atlanta, just once......I want to go to England, Paris, and Italy, and The Galapagos Island."

About that time in 2007, *The Atlanta Journal* newspaper ran a story offering free training for the race, and a free entrance fee if you wrote a story about why you wanted to run the race. So, I wrote the paper and explained, "I was born in Atlanta and had always wanted to try to run the race." They liked my story, and I was in! At that time I was 67 and wasn't even a walker, much less a runner! So, in March of that year I started walking every day, and my techie husband sent me off with an MP3 player, sunscreen, a hat, and a step-counter. I got better, but not really good enough. Still, it was exciting to know that it was too late to back out, and I *was* going to finish—not running all the time, but walking some, running some, and accepting water along the way, which I poured over my head.

I was amazed at some of the people who participated. Some were handicapped in some way and just walked very slowly but finished. There were groups of people having a great time doing it together. Along the way, as we passed the big Catholic Church in Buckhead, the priest was standing there with a bucket of water—I'm assuming holy water?—saying, "God Bless You" as he threw water at us.

After crossing the finish line, I got the coveted tee shirt, something many Atlantans have from every year before. I was very sore and walked in a bent over position for about three days, but I got to check off #4 on my list. I didn't become a great runner or go on to run marathons, but running it once was what it was all about for me.

Don't even ask what my time was.

LYNNE CROSSING THE PEACHTREE ROAD RACE FINISH LINE, 2007

CHAPTER 33

The Dunwoody Preservation Trust

After graduation, a whole new world opened up to me. I was able to combine my real estate experience and my love for historic preservation, and specialize in historic homes and properties. "Throw me in the Briar Patch!" Note, this phrase is Southern, was taken from *The Tales of Uncle Remus* by Joel Chandler Harris, and was said by Brer Rabbit who loved being in the briar patch. It means "Toss me into my happy place!"

My dear friend Joyce Amacher, an outstanding community volunteer in our City of Dunwoody and coincidentally my son's mother-in-law, encouraged me to research the remaining historic homes which remained in Dunwoody. Along with the Dunwoody Homeowners Association, we also founded the Dunwoody Preservation Trust. Later, an opportunity arose for Dunwoody to attempt to save the Cheek-Spruill

House, a very important early 1900s house right in the middle of Dunwoody. A group of like-minded people joined the Dunwoody Preservation Trust, Inc. We made our first project saving this precious house that we considered the Crown Jewel of Dunwoody. The deed to the house was presented to the Dunwoody Preservation Trust at the Dunwoody Fourth of July parade in 1998. Later, it became the first house in Dunwoody that I put on the National Register of Historic Places.

THE DUNWOODY FARMHOUSE BEFORE RESTORATION

The Cheek-Spruill House, circa 1906-1907, is classified as a "gabled ell" house, had been lived in by Carey Spruill and his wife for 43 years. Mr. Spruill had a large cornfield just East of his house which faced Mt. Vernon Road. He farmed this cornfield for many years, as Dunwoody's shopping malls, stores and houses were built. It was quite a sight to drive by in modern times to see him plowing a row of corn with "Shorty", his mule. He would plow a row with an old fashioned wooden plow, and when he came to the end of the row, he and "Shorty" would go out into Mt. Vernon Road and stop traffic so he could turn "Shorty" around and get back on his land for the next row. One day, we didn't see him in the cornfield and everyone was worried. So we called the house to check on him, and asked him if everything was okay. Mr. Spruill said, "Shorty died." Mr. Spruill himself died in 1983, and when Mrs. Florence Spruill died in 1994, the Trust immediately contacted the two surviving sons, Hugh and Edwin. They gave us the time to try to save the Farmhouse, and we will be forever grateful.

Only family had been allowed to go into the Farmhouse for many years, and so interest was high to see it and save it. The first thing we did was to have an "Open House" before the campaign began, so that people could see what needed to be done. We also had a "Hug the House Day. We encircled the house with a yellow caution-tape, and all of us joined hands and danced around the house singing *The Farmer in the Dell*. Yes, I know it sounds funny, but we wanted the people of Dunwoody to feel that it would belong to them if we could save it.

Joyce and I pulled some unbelievable pranks and tricks to try and save what is now known as "The Dunwoody Farmhouse." My brother Larry had t-shirts made for us to sell to raise funds with a picture of the Dunwoody Farmhouse on the front. Joyce and I took an extra-large t-shirt and both put it on together. This picture of us "joined at the hip" is one of my favorites, showing not only the Farmhouse, but how close we are as friends!

LYNNE AND JOYCE "JOINED AT THE HIP," 1997

DUNWOODY CRIER FRONT PAGE, PAINTING BY BOB CARGILL, 1996

THE FARMHOUSE WAS SAVED!

We talked watercolor artist Bob Cargill into painting us a picture of an all-night gas station which would be built on the corner where the Farmhouse was located. Dick Williams, owner and editor of our local newspaper, *The Crier*, put it on the front page. The headline was, "Dunwoody Farmhouse Replaced by All Night Gas Station." And underneath the picture in very small letters, it read, "Unless you help save it." We stood out in the middle of Chamblee-Dunwoody, our major road, with a sign that read, "Save Me" with the Farmhouse in the background.

Dunwoody came together in a way that it had not before, and it was saved So, of course, Joyce and I stood out in the road again with the house in the background with a sign that read, "Thank You!"

RENOVATED FARMHOUSE

The Dunwoody Preservation Trust (www.dunwoodypreservationtrust.org) was founded in 1994. Joyce Amacher and I served as its first co-presidents for 10 years.

CHAPTER 34

Church Drama

Our church has a wonderful Artistic Director, Robert Edwards, who treats us to plays throughout the year. I had added "Be in a play" to my Bucket List. At the time, Robert was beginning rehearsals for the musical play "Joseph and The Amazing Technicolor Dream Coat."

I told Robert, "I have a Bucket List, and I only have two things left. Do you have any part I can play in 'Joseph?'"

Robert said, "Sure, I think you could be an angel, and also play another part involving 'Little Bo Peep.'"

This role was a part in the play where Robert took some license and had Bo Peep leading her sheep when Joseph's brothers attacked the sheep, which had the entire flock represented simply by a stuffed toy sheep on a board with wheels.

The cast had the most wonderful time doing this show, and it was a real joy to check off #5.

Later, I tap danced in *Anything Goes*, another one of Robert's productions. I had one line: "Who is he?"

Joseph and The Amazing Technicolor Dream Coat, WITH LYNNE, FAR LEFT, 2008

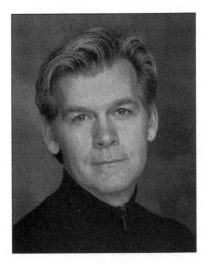

ROBERT EDWARDS, ARTISTIC DIRECTOR,
DUNWOODY UNITED METHODIST CHURCH

BO PEEP

ANYTHING GOES, 2015

CHAPTER 35

Fabulous Trips

Over the years, we traveled to England, once by ourselves to stay with family friends, and once with my brother Larry and his wife, Colleen. The second trip with them involved switching houses with a family. We met the English family at the Atlanta airport, and they stayed in our house for three weeks, fed our pets, and drove our car. In turn, we stayed in their house, fed their kitties, and drove their car. Everybody asked me if we knew them beforehand, and yes, there was a connection through Noah's uncle who had been in England during the War.

Colleen had many friends who traveled, and so we tried our best to see everything. The husband of the English family staying in our house was a "Bobbie" (policeman) in London, and he arranged for us to see things we ordinarily would not have seen.

NOAH AND LYNNE WITH THE BOBBIES IN LONDON, ENGLAND, AUGUST 1992

LYNNE AND COLEEN IN THE "STOCKS" WITH LARRY

AND NOAH, COTSWOLDS, AUGUST 1992

Larry and Colleen had to leave after two weeks and get back home to Miami where Colleen's parents were staying with the children. We stayed on another week and went to the South of England where I planned to do my research on the trug baskets. We were sitting in a tavern shortly after we got there, and the owner had the TV on. He asked if we were from the states, and we said yes, and he said "Aren't you glad you aren't from Miami, Florida?" Then we looked at the TV which showed an airplane upside down on the tarmac, a result of Hurricane Andrew. So Larry and Colleen got home just in time to board up the house and gather together as family with Colleen's Mom and Dad. Unfortunately, their house was in the eye of the terrible hurricane, and it tore the roof off the house, dumped their furniture into their swimming pool, and ended up displacing the family for a long time.

Another fabulous trip was with my son David and a friend to Paris. This was an unbelievable trip for us and was a 33rd anniversary present from Dave. He and his friend Bev ran a half-marathon while we were there and got a medal. We stayed at the Sacre Coeur Hotel in the same room where Picasso had once lived. So #6, #7, and #8 were checked off the Bucket List.

The Galapagos Island is very probably not going to be checked off the list, mainly because of Noah's health. But that's okay. I've made another list which will keep me near home.

PARIS, MARCH 2009

VIEW FROM OUR ROOM

DAVE AND FRIEND BEV IN MONTMARTE

CELEBRATING OUR 33RD ANNIVERSARY WITH
MUSTACHES THAT LYNNE BROUGHT ALONG.

CHAPTER 36

Precious Pets

We have been blessed with the most wonderful pets. They have been like our children. When Noah and I got married, we would have had a baby together, but we had both been "fixed." So our pets were our babies. The hardest part is when they got old and had to leave. But it is still better than us going first and leaving them behind.

The first pet we had was a beautiful Sheltie named Brandy. He was sent to us just before our wedding by Larry and Colleen, and we picked him up at the airport. He was such a good boy! Unfortunately, while we were on our honeymoon, brother Dave was taking care of him, and he escaped from the house and was run over by a car. Dave called us while we were at Mammoth Cave and gave us the news. He felt so badly about it, but those things happen. Poor Dave had to bury him in the yard of the Spalding Drive house, along with other birds, hamsters, and assorted small pets that the boys had buried over the years.

BRANDY, 1979

The second pet Noah and I had was a dachshund puppy that we named Horace. We decided that Horace needed a playmate, so we went to look for a girl, and I said to Noah, "But what if we can't find a cute one?" This became a family joke; have you *ever* seen an ugly puppy? So we found Heidi and brought her home.

We both worked, and when we got home at night, those two little rascals had always gotten into some trouble. Together, they were able to rip the wallpaper off the kitchen wall by biting the bottom and then backing up. We ended up advertising them free if someone would take them both because they were in love.

HORACE AND HEIDI, 1980

The third pet we had was Tim or Timmy Boy. We think that if God wants you to have a cat, he will send one to you. So, Tim showed up one day. He lived to be twelve. Tim was the best cat ever, and he was greatly loved by the neighbors and their children. We were known as "Tim's parents." Noah built Tim a pet door, complete on the outside of the house with his own house number: 1125-1/2 Spalding Drive. He was an indoor/outdoor cat, so he didn't need a litter box. He had the run of the house and slept wherever he wanted to, but was sure to wake us up in the morning by sitting on my stomach and putting his nose on my nose.

He liked to bring in moles, chipmunks, and tiny baby bunnies through his little door. Noah got to be great at catching them with an upside down trash can. One time Tim pulled a trick when Larry and Colleen and their kids were visiting. We were eating dinner, and Colleen said, "What's that squeaking noise?" And I said, "It's probably a bird on the patio." About that time, Tim came in through his door with four pink feet hanging out of his mouth. Colleen and daughter Stirling stood up on the chairs and shrieked, upon which Tim dropped the mole, earning him the Barfield name of "Mole Breath."

When Tim died, I wrapped him in one of my night gowns that he especially loved and put him in a wooden box; we buried him in the "South 40" in back of our house on Spalding. We had a small monument made for him, and the rumor in the neighborhood was that there was a person buried in our back yard.

DEBBIE WITH TIM, 1985

Shortly after Tim died we asked our vet what kind of dog he would recommend for us, and he suggested a toy poodle for our fourth pet. We had planned on naming a boy toy poodle Clifford after my grandfather, and if we chose a girl, we would call her Abbie Lucille after my grandmother. We later found out that my grandmother's name was Mollie, not Abbie, but by then the poodle had the name.

NOAH WITH ABBIE, SPALDING DRIVE, 1996

While I was at an Anthropology Conference at Jekyll Island, Noah went poodle shopping, and the first little puppy who ran to him was Abbie. She was solid black as a puppy, and as she grew older, she became a pretty brown color called *café au lait*. Abbie lived to be sixteen years old. I still have her picture on the piano in her Christmas outfit. I'll take it down when I'm good and ready!

Our fifth pet is our gorgeous, smart, white Siamese/Persian mix kitty, Mia, a.k.a. Fluffy. She was a rescue, and we heard about her from Barbara and Bob Farmer who set up an appointment for us to see her. So, we think of Barb and Bob as her grandparents.

MIA, ALSO KNOWN AS FLUFFY, APRIL 2011

She sheds *all* of the time. There are white hairs everywhere, but she is so worth it! It is my exercise routine to pick up, vacuum, and scout out all of the fur. We will supply you with a lint roller if you come to visit, because you WILL leave with some "bunny fur". She talks all the time the way Siamese cats do, and by certain sounds, we know if she is purring, wants treats, water, or to go outside on a pretty day. We have to stay with her outside as she is very skittish about cars coming down the street, or—Heaven forbid!—there's a dog!

CHAPTER 37

Very Special Family and Friends

My love and a very special thank you to my dear cousin, Billie Barfield Sheffield who has acted as Historian for the Barfield-Eason Family, and to my dear cousin, Sadie Ann Lacy Johnson, who has acted as Historian for the Moore-Lacy Family.

BILLIE BARFIELD SHEFFIELD, 2013

223

SADIE AND GLENN JOHNSON, 1999

COUSINS (STANDING L-R) PEARL BARFIELD, BILLIE BARFIELD SHEFFIELD,
BOBBIE BARFIELD SHERROD, (SEATED) LYNNE BARFIELD BYRD,
CAROL COLLINS AT MIMI'S IN PERIMETER MALL, DUNWOODY, 2014

BILLIE AND BOBBIE'S GRANDCHILDREN, SEATTLE, WASHINGTON,
2004: DREW SHERROD, ADDISON ROPER, BEN WILDER,
GRIFFIN ROPER, RORY SHERROD, McKENNA SHERROD

BEE AND HONEY BARFIELD WITH THEIR GIRLS BOBBIE AND BILLIE

THREE SILLY COUSINS: LYNNE, BOBBIE AND BILLIE, 2014

JOYCE AND BILL AMACHER ON THE BENCH AT BROOK RUN
PARK DEDICATED TO JOYCE, MARCH 21, 2015

JOYCE WITH SON ZACK, GRANDDAUGHTERS KIMBERLY AND ALLISON AND DAUGHTER-IN-LAW AMIE AMACHER, BROOK RUN PARK, MARCH 21, 2015

LYNNE AND JOYCE'S GRANDDAUGHTERS, BRENDA, 5, AND SAMANTHA, 7, WEARING SOME OF JOYCE'S HATS AND JEWELRY

NOAH'S GREAT GRANDDAUGHTER BAILEE, 6, AND GRANDDAUGHTER SARAH

CRAWFORD, VISITING FROM RIFLE, COLORADO, 2015

(RIGHT) NOAH'S GREAT GRANDDAUGHTER MARLEE, 2

NOAH'S BROTHER, RALPH AND WIFE, JEANNIE, MARCH 2015

"THE WIVES CLUB": DUSTY, LYNNE, AND BARBARA VISITING
NOAH'S MOTHER AT HER HOME, AROUND 2002

BARBARA THEUS, LYNNE AND MARY ANN BEAUFAIT, CELEBRATING MANY
YEARS OF BIRTHDAYS TOGETHER AT LA MADELEINE'S, JUNE 25, 1984

RALPH, HELPING WITH CHRISTMAS DINNER ON SPALDING, 1996

GRADUATION DAY, GEORGIA STATE UNIVERSITY, LYNNE WITH
GRANDDAUGHTERS SARAH AND SAMANTHA, JUNE 25, 1996

ANNUAL BREAKFAST WITH THE THEUSES, THE BEAUFAITS, AND THE
BYRDS AT 57TH FIGHTER SQUADRON RESTAURANT EVERY JANUARY, 2005

NOAH TAKES AN ULTRALITE RIDE IN KEY WEST
ON HIS 60TH BIRTHDAY, MAY 21, 1998

DAVE AND FRIEND BEV CARVER HEAD OUT FOR A RAINY MARATHON
IN ATLANTA, NOVEMBER 2012 WHILE VISITING FROM COLORADO

AUNT BEE CUTS THE ANNIVERSARY CAKE FOR HER
AND HONEY'S 77TH CELEBRATION.

BEE, "THE SCRABBLE QUEEN" AND BOBBIE PLAYING

LYNNE, JANICE, AND NANCY ON A GETAWAY TRIP
TO HELEN, GEORGIA, AROUND 1974

FAST FRIENDS FOR A LONG TIME: MARY ANN
BEAUFAIT, LYNNE, BARBARA THEUS

LESLIE PERRY AND LYNNE AT ANTHROPOLOGY
CONFERENCE IN AUGUSTA, GEORGIA, 1993

FOUR GENERATIONS: (L-R) JOYCE, SARA PATRICK, ZELDA, LYNNE (HOLDING SAMANTHA), AND JOYCE'S MOTHER IN JOYCE'S KITCHEN, MAY 10, 1985

GREAT GRANNY SARA PATRICK, NOAH, AND BABY SAMANTHA, 6 MONTHS OLD, 1985

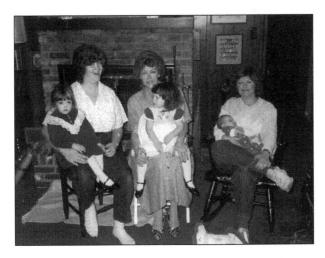

ZELDA (WITH SAMANTHA), GRANDMOTHER JOYCE (WITH
LAUREN), AND ZERAH (WITH ELLIOTT), CHRISTMAS 1988

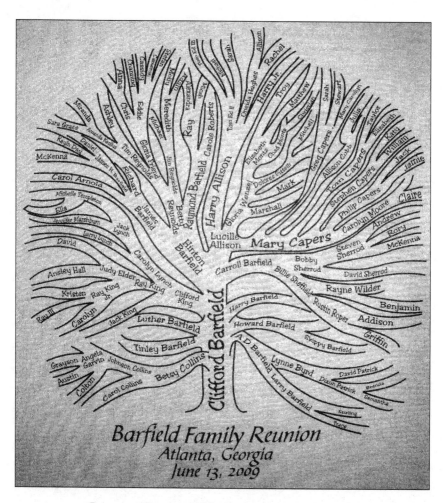

Barfield Family Reunion
Atlanta, Georgia
June 13, 2009

BARFIELD REUNION T-SHIRT DESIGNED BY LYNNE'S

BROTHER, LARRY BARFIELD, JUNE 13, 2009

The Bella Literati Book Club

In 1986, several friends who love to read—Barbara Theus, Julie Post, Marene Emanuel, Chris Lindsey, Mary Ann Beaufait, and I—started the Bella Literati Book Club. We didn't name it at first, but in a couple of years, we decided on Bella Literati, which we thought sounded like "The Beautiful Intellectuals." In 2016, we will celebrate our 30th anniversary.

Through the years, people have come and gone, but this core group has remained. We are all very different and have enjoyed reading very different books as each member takes a turn choosing the selection. We started meeting at each other's homes at night, once a month, but now we meet at one member's house which is central to all of us, and we meet on a Sunday afternoon instead of driving at night.

We have had many fun events. I think probably our favorite was the Winter Fairy Festival in 1996, which took place at our house on Spalding Drive. There was magic in the air! The request was that everybody come dressed as a fairy of their choice. One of our members, Marene, came dressed as Liberace. She said, "You didn't say what *kind* of fairy!" She had rented a Liberace costume complete with gold candelabra. I had strung Christmas lights all over the dining room and living room. We all brought a dish, and one of the girls brought an amazing delicious cake from her favorite bakery. One girl threw fairy dust, and a fairy wand was given to each of the Bellas, recognizing each member as a bonafide fairy. After a bit of wine, we all went in the woodsy backyard and danced around, no doubt giving the neighbors an "eye full."

Another favorite was our Solstice of the Goddesses Festival held at Barbara Theus' house in the red hot summer of 1996. We all had to use one sheet to make our costumes. I was the goddess of costume jewelry, and I had pinned most of my costume pins on my "unbreathable" no-iron sheet. Talk about *hot!* We all had to share something like a poem or funny story under the scarf tent we had constructed above us on ropes. I shared my proposal from Noah via a recorder. Fun! We all brought food and laid it all out in the middle of the tent.

Words can't express how much this book club has meant to me. We have been through marriages and divorces, changing careers, the death of parents, sickness, bad boyfriends for some, and many other things, and have always been there for each other. More than once, I have doubted that I could accomplish something, and more than once, the Book Club convinced me to try something new.

A big Thank You to my dear Book Club. Mwah! Mwah! Mwah!

FAIRY FESTIVAL MAGIC LUNCH, LYNNE'S HOME, 1994

THE FAIRIES RECEIVE THEIR WANDS, 1994

BELLA LITERATI SOLSTICE OF THE GODDESSES FESTIVAL, 1996

THE SOLSTICE OF THE GODDESSES, AT BARBARA'S HOME, 1996

THE FIRST SOCIAL EVENT, BEFORE RESTORATION,
AT THE DUNWOODY FARMHOUSE, 1997

BARBARA THEUS WITH "FRIEND" PANDA BEAR, AT HER HOME, 2000

BELLA HALLOWEEN PARTY AT JULIE POST'S HOME, MARIETTA, 2001

THE BELLAS AT THE CHIHULY GLASS EXHIBIT AT THE
ATLANTA BOTANICAL GARDENS, OCTOBER 2004

SLEEP-OVER TO CELEBRATE OUR 20TH ANNIVERSARY IN THE BREGENZER
COTTAGE AT THE HISTORIC WOODALL HOUSE, DUNWOODY, ONLY
TO FIND OUT THAT IT WAS THE 19TH ANNIVERSARY, 2007

BELLAS CELEBRATE THE "BOATING PARTY" AT BERKELEY LAKE, SUMMER 2009

Eileen Barrow, Berkeley Lake hostess, Summer 2009

Maureen Emmanuel and Mary Ann Beaufait, Dillard trip, 2012

CHRIS LINDSEY ANTIQUING IN DILLARD, AUGUST 2012

JULIE POST AND CHRIS LINDSEY AT DILLARD COTTAGE, 2012

CHAPTER 38

Looking Ahead

I n Georgia, you can go to school free if you are over 62 years old, so after my retirement in April of 2015, I made a new Bucket List. I'm not sure about the whole list yet—losing weight is on there somewhere—but I am going back to the same Community College where I first started in 1983.

In many ways, I have a strong sense of "Going backwards in order to go into the future." I am also a strong proponent of the "School of Why Not?" Even though I am 76, my friend Pitta said to me once, "Age is just a number!"

Georgia Perimeter College, a branch of the University System of Georgia, was called DeKalb College in the 1980s. As of January 2016, it will become a satellite of Georgia State University. This will make it the largest college in Georgia with over 54,000 students and will include all of the other satellite Georgia Perimeter College campuses surrounding the Greater Atlanta area.

I have to say that there are quite a few hoops to go through to be admitted when you are older, but it is possible. There is help available.

Ms. Judith Nichols at Georgia Perimeter College teamed me up with Dr. Wayne Paul and Dr. Steve Benton, advisors at the college to whom I am indebted for their patience and interest in helping me. Unless a potential student is working on a Ph.D.—which I am *not*—one can get credit for undergraduate courses already taken if they fit the completion criteria of the Associate Degree. Dr. Paul checked with the Registrar to help me plan a track for an Associate in English, which will include Creative Writing, Public Speaking, and quite a lot of literature that I'm looking forward to. Older adults can choose to audit a course if they wish, but I want to be in the classroom and be held accountable for studying and taking the tests because this will keep me honest. The classroom experience gives me the opportunity to work with the other students, which I have always loved. I'll ask the Book Club if they think I can do it, and I know what they will say! I can now read all I want to, have fun with Noah, and do things we both want to do. Also, I'll keep up with friends and family more and send inspirational things to the grandchildren and great grandchildren.

At this point, the Chestnut House and Farm, known on the National Register as The Donaldson-Bannister House and Farm is in dire need of restoration. Although it has been saved, it is owned by the City of Dunwoody and is considered to be a park. However, it must be cared for, and maintained, and there is very little money available to restore it. Preservation is not cheap. These wonderful properties from our past give us our nostalgic sense of place and must pay their own way somehow or be supported with public/private funds. Otherwise, they will suffer what preservationists call "demolition by neglect." In addition, the Theater at Brook Run Park, also known as The Liane Levitan Park, is deteriorating at an alarming rate and will need a lot of restoration. At this point, it is in danger of being torn down by the City with the land to be re-used as "the great lawn." A group of us, headed up by President Danny Ross of The Brook Run Conservancy, are trying to save it. These are things that would be of interest to me as community projects. Both of these worthy properties belong to the City of Dunwoody, and I want to participate in saving them.

CHAPTER 39

Staying Strong

Here's my favorite prayer, "The Radical Prayer" by Flora Slosson Wuellner from her book *Prayer, Stress and Our Inner Wounds*. I first saw it on the bulletin board of a very special friend, Bob Allgood, a gentleman at Roswell United Methodist Church and a retired Colonel in the Army. He has used it many times in many situations.

> The Radical Prayer is a special form of prayer, extraordinarily helpful when I am perplexed about a moral decision or direction for myself. I called it "the radical prayer":
>
> Holy Spirit, if this is right for me, let it become more firmly rooted and established in my life. If this is

wrong for me, let it become less important to me, and let it be increasingly removed from my life.

We should not pray this prayer unless we mean it. It is always heard and answered in definite and surprising ways. Habits begin to lose their grip. Relationships change. Neglected parts of our selves begin to grow. New attractions and likings surface. Surprising abilities appear. Some familiar old tendencies become unattractive to us. Something always happens when we pray this prayer in honesty.

LYNNE, 75, AND NOAH, 76, IN CHURCH DIRECTORY,
DUNWOODY UNITED METHODIST, 2014

And now, here's some advice that has worked for me:

Play to your strengths and not your weaknesses.

Don't let the sun set on a Thank You note.

You have built-in coping skills. Use them and re-frame your bad days and what you consider "bad luck" into "good luck."

If you are feeling depressed, try laughing or crying it off, or participate in an enjoyable, regular exercise program. Keep trying until you really like the one you pick and keep doing it even after you feel better.

It is quite all right to yell and scream at God. He can take it. It's okay to throw dishes also, just not at someone.

Don't give away your deviled egg plate.

Being a good neighbor is not about whom he/she is. It's about who you are.

Make lists. My cousin Bobbie taught me this. Plan your day, and your life, but leave room for the unexpected happening.

Mama said, "If you can't say something nice, don't say anything at all."

Don't curse. Instead, say things like, "Well, cut off my legs and call me 'Shorty.'" My granddaughters love this one.

Do some kind of service for your community.

If you are a spiritual person, visit places of worship until you find the one you just love, and then be an active participant in helping them spread what you have found.

Bless Your Heart, Lynne

Acknowledgements

Love and thanks, first and always, to my husband Noah for his never ending love, patience, and kindness, not only for his help with this book, but mainly for sticking with me for thirty-six years. I would also like to thank our children, Dixon, David, and Debbie.

My gratitude to my trusted editor Wayne South Smith without whom I could not have pulled this book together. Our Atlanta roots made communication easy, and it was fun to work together.

I also want to thank the wonderful Morningside Mothers; you are all gone now, but I will see you again. Thanks, too, to all the teachers who took an interest in me.

Heartfelt appreciation to my dear friends of many years Janice, Nancy, Annetta and Virginia who are a big part of this book and my life. And, of course, I extend this to my cousins Billie, Bobbie, Carol, Pearl, Sadie Ann, and Bettie Lou, who have shared my life story.

A special thank you to Joyce Amacher, who taught me many wise things about life and was my co-author of *The Story of Dunwoody, 1975-2001.*

Also love and a special thank you to the girls in the Bella Literati Book Club, which has thrived for 30 years! They have encouraged me and taught me to live joyously!

And Praise to God for my abundant blessings, not the least of which is having been born in the South.

About the Author

Lynne Byrd was born in Atlanta, Georgia and raised in the Morningside and Virginia Highlands neighborhoods. She attended Morningside Elementary and graduated from Grady High School in 1957. She has a B.A. in Anthropology and a Master's in Historic Preservation, both degrees from Georgia State University.

Following Mrs. Ethel Warren Spruill and Mrs. Elizabeth Lockhart Davis's book, *The Story of Dunwoody: Its Heritage and Horizons, 1821-1975*, originally published in 1975, Byrd and co-author Joyce Amacher wrote the city's history from 1975-2001. Both are combined into one book, *The Story of Dunwoody, 1821-2001*, which is currently in print.

Byrd has listed three Dunwoody houses on the National Register of Historic Places: The Cheek-Spruill House, a.k.a. the Dunwoody Farmhouse, c. 1906-1907; The Donaldson-Bannister House, c. 1866, and The Isaac Roberts House, c. 1895.

Byrd served a ten-year term as the first co-president of the Dunwoody Preservation Trust, alongside friend Joyce Amacher. She has also served on the DeKalb County Historic Preservation Commission.

Lynne Byrd and her husband, Noah, have enjoyed thirty years in real estate together, with Lynne specializing in her beloved historic properties. They live in Dunwoody and enjoy collecting antiques, reading, watching movies, and working with non-profits who encourage preservation.

Made in the USA
Lexington, KY
29 September 2015